Joyce Kling
Tina Dorthe Nielsen

Denmark for Foreign Students and Faculty

HANDELSHØJSKOLENS FORLAG
Copenhagen Business School Press

Denmark for Foreign Students and Faculty

© Handelshøjskolens Forlag, *Copenhagen Business School Press*, 1999
Cover designed by Kontrapunkt
Illustrated by Lars Larsen
Set in ITC Stone Serif by ABK-Sats, Copenhagen
Printed by Reproset, Copenhagen
1. edition 1999

ISBN 87-16-13362-5

Distribution:

Scandinavia
Munksgaard/DBK, Siljangade 2-8, P.O. Box 1731
DK-2300 Copenhagen S, Denmark
phone: +45 3269 7788, fax: +45 3269 7789

North America
Copenhagen Business School Press
Books International Inc.
P.O. Box 605
Hendon, VA 20172-0605, USA
phone: +1 703 661 1500, fax: +1 703 661 1501
E-mail: intpubmkt@aol.com

Rest of the World
Marston Book Services, P.O. Box 269
Abingdon, Oxfordshire, OX14 4YN, UK
phone: +44 (0) 1235 465500, fax: +44 (0) 1235 465555
E-mail Direct Customers: direct.order@marston.co.uk
E-mail Booksellers: trade.order@marston.co.uk

All rights reserved. No part of this publication may be reproduced or used in any form or by any means - graphic, electronic or mecanical including photocopying, recording, taping or information storage or retrieval systems - without permission in writing from Handelshøjskolens Forlag, *Copenhagen Business School Press*, Nansensgade 19, DK 1366 Copenhagen, Denmark

Contents

Acknowledgements *7*
Introduction *9*
Highlights in Denmark's History *11*
Danish Society *17*
Higher Education *25*
Social Life at Danish Universities *33*
Practical Matters *43*
Making Social Connections *61*
Voices of Experience *73*
Appendix 1. Traditional and Legal Holidays *85*
Appendix 2. Royal Danish Embassies and Consulates *89*
Appendix 3. Institutions of Higher Education *98*
Appendix 4. Accomodations *109*
Appendix 5. Glossary *111*
References *113*

Acknowledgements

We would like to take this opportunity to thank everyone who generously gave his or her time and input for this book. We would first like to thank Lauge Stetting for giving us the opportunity to take this to press. This project has been a long time in the making and Lauge's patience and input have been greatly appreciated. In particular, we thank Robin Jensen from the International Office at the Copenhagen Business School (CBS) for her comments and feedback on the early drafts of the book. We owe a debt of gratitude to Robin and her staff at CBS for their initial work on the school's Copenhagen Survival Guide for exchange students. In addition, we would like to thank the Danish Ministry of Education and the secretariat at the Danish Rectors' Conference for answering all of our questions and queries. Lastly, we thank our families for supporting us in our efforts and waiting patiently on the weekends for us to come home.

Joyce Kling
Tina Dorthe Nielsen

Copenhagen, Denmark
May 1999

Introduction

So you are going to be in Denmark for six months, a year, or perhaps a three-year stay. You have heard Denmark described as the land of castles and mermaids, fairytales and pastry, and architecture and butter cookies. But you know there is more that you need to find out about the world you are about to enter. Although the stereotypes do exist and are real pieces of the jigsaw puzzle that makes up Denmark, the tiny nation on the southern edge of Scandinavia, there is much more under the surface – much more than just sightseeing and picture postcards.

Whether you are trying to decide to take the leap or have already accepted a position at a Danish institution, you are most likely full of questions about what Denmark is really like, what are the Danes all about or just how you will cope with the being a guest in a foreign land. The purpose of this book is to give you some insights into what makes Denmark unique. This is not a tourist guidebook but a practical handbook.

While in Denmark, you will be confronted with the Danes and their habits, some more unique than others. Daily rituals will be different than to what you are accustomed. We hope you will find these differences enchanting. Too often cultural difference lead to stress and discomfort. The information presented here will help to alleviate some of the stress that comes when you move to a new country where you do not speak the language or even recognize some of the food. The book contains information to help prepare before you leave home as well as useful tips and advice to assist you during your stay.

You will find between the covers of this book both facts and advice to help you answer some of the questions that have faced other foreigners in Denmark. You will find a bit of historical information to shed some light on what has gone into the development of the national mentality and the educational system. You will find basic information on banking, shopping and taxes. You will find addresses and Internet sites to assist you in your search for more specific information in your field. But mostly, you will find suggestions to help you in the more obscure areas of Danish life – suggestions to help you feel a little bit more comfortable both academically and socially. We hope that armed with this information, you will be able to get all you desire out of your stay in Denmark.

Living in a foreign country can be a surprising and incredibly rewarding and educational experience. This guide should take some of the challenge out of being a foreigner and assist you in your work and studies.

We wish you all the best and good luck in Denmark.

Highlights in Denmark's History

In order to understand Denmark and the Danes it is important to get a sense of the nation's past. Denmark has a long history which has made for wonderful adventure stories. For such a small nation, Denmark has left its mark on the pages of world history. Below are a few highlights.

The early years ...
The first historical reference to Denmark as a nation can be found on runic stones found in the town of Jelling in Jutland. Stones dating back to around 958 AD make references to King Harald's victorious battle for Denmark. Since that time, the country has been a kingdom. By the year 1000, the Danish Vikings had made a name for themselves pillaging and plundering across northern Europe. At one time they even reigned over England and Scotland.

Leading up to around 1500, Denmark was busy fighting many battles with neighboring countries. Legend tells us that during one of these battles in Estonia (1219), "*Dannebrog*" – the Danish flag – fell down from heaven.

In 1479, a few years before Columbus is said to have discovered America, the University of Copenhagen was founded.

1500-1800
1536 brought the reformation to Denmark replacing Catholicism with Protestantism. Approximately 50 years later King

Christian IV was born. Christian IV left his mark on the nation in the form of the numerous buildings which were constructed under his reign. Among some of his architectural achievements were castles, housing for the navy and their families, housing for students and the remarkable Roundtower (Rundetårn) in the heart of the capital. Christian IV also led the country into a 30-year war in which Denmark lost a large chunk of land to Sweden. The high construction and military costs naturally took their toll on Denmark and upon his death in 1648, Christian IV left Denmark on the verge of financial disaster.

In the beginning of the 18th century times were very bad for Danish agriculture. The landowners sought out ways to keep the peasants down. The King came to the aid of the landowners in 1735 with a proclamation, which stated that male peasants between the ages of 14 and 36 were legally bound to the estate on which they were born and were forbidden to leave the territory. Thus, the landowners were guaranteed workers. In 1788, at approximately the same time as the French revolution, this proclamation was abolished. To commemorate the moment, a statue of liberty *Frihedsstøtten,* was placed in central Copenhagen, close to what is now the central station.

The government realized that areas other than just agriculture needed to be developed. Thus, the government began to give aid to the tradespeople and manufacturers. During the 1730's, several houses of trade and industry established themselves. These companies purchased raw materials from overseas and produced goods for the Danish market. Each company was even granted a monopoly on their primary goods. By utilizing raw materials drawn from the colonies, Denmark was able to maximize productivity and benefit economically from these territories.

1800-1900

In 1807, the British navy bombed Copenhagen heavily since neutral Denmark did not want to go into alliance with them. Instead, Denmark aligned with France and thus went to war with England. Due to Denmark's alliance with Napoleon, most European countries were considered enemies of Denmark. Even Denmark's neighbor, Sweden, attacked the little land. Denmark was defeated and in the peace treaty of January 1814, Denmark was forced to give up Norway to Sweden.

Since 1814, there has been compulsory education for Danish children, a right stated in the constitution.

Concurrently, 1814 marked a milestone year in terms of education in Denmark. A new law introduced compulsory education for every Danish child. This principle remains intact and is printed in the Danish constitution.

Among the renowned Danes of this time period are H. C. Ørsted (1777-1851), scientist and discoverer of electromagnetism, Søren Kierkegaard (1813-1855), philosopher and existentialist, and of course, H. C. Andersen (1805-1875), the world's most beloved writer of children's stories and fairytales. H. C. Ørsted laid the foundations for the study of engineering in Denmark by taking the initiative in the establishment of the Polytechnical Institute in 1829. Taking a different scientific approach, J. C. Jakobsen (1811-1887) satisfied his own ambitions and the thirst of the Danes with the founding of the Carlsberg brewery (named for his son Carl).

In the 1840s, a new type of school with a target population

of adults was established. In a sense, these schools sought to bring the nation together by educating the population in areas of nationalism and public spirit. These schools became known as *højskoler*. Eventually, these schools expanded their curriculum to meet the ever growing need to the Danish population. Niels Frederik Severin Grundtvig is considered the founding father of the *højskole* movement in Denmark. Since Grundtvig's time, *højskoler* have remained a vital part of Danish continuing education.

On June 5, 1849 (known today as Constitution Day), Kong Frederik VII gave in to pressure from different interest groups in society and allowed Denmark a free constitution. This date marked the end of Denmark's absolute monarchy and the beginning of the constitutional monarchy. At that time, Denmark established a two-chambered parliament.

During the last quarter of the 19th century, Danish agriculture refined their production and the exportation of butter and bacon. The great success Denmark experienced with this exportation can be credited not only to the improved products that were sold, but also to the extent to which the dairies and slaughterhouses were owned cooperatively by the farmers, thus greatly improving the productive capability of small holders as well as the standard of living. The cooperative movement's roots can be traced back to Grundtvig's *højskole* movement.

The 1900s

At the beginning of the 20th century many major things occurred in Denmark. In particular, Niels Bohr (1885-1962) presented his theory of the hydrogen atom in 1913, at the age of 27. At approximately the same time, Danish women gained their right to vote through a change in the constitution in 1915.

Although World War I commenced without the Danes entering into the war, the Treaty of Versailles affected Denmark geographically. The treaty stated that the people in the southern part of Jutland, which had been lost to Germany during wars in the 19th century, could vote on whether they wanted to belong to Denmark again. In the early months of 1920 the people in the former Danish region voted that Southern Jutland should return to Denmark. Later that year King Christian X symbolically crossed the border from the north on a white horse and Southern Jutland was then reunited with the rest of the country.

During World War II, Denmark was occupied by Hitler's army for five long years and was liberated on the evening of May 4, 1945. (Danes commemorate this day by placing candles in the windows.) Four years later Denmark became a member of NATO.

The Danish constitution was changed in 1953 so that the parliament now consists of just one chamber. In connection with this, a law was introduced that allowed a woman to lead the monarchy and be heir to the throne.

In January of 1972, King Frederik IX passed away and his oldest daughter, Crown-Princess Margrethe became Queen Margrethe II and was the first female sovereign since Margrethe I reigned in the 14th century.

Denmark entered into the EEC on January 1, 1973. Although the country joined the community at that time with a two-thirds vote of approval, EEC and later EU referendums require quite a bit of debate and discussion within the Danish society. At the present time, Denmark is an active member in the EU but has voted to remain on the periphery in certain matters, for example European currency, the euro.

In the summer of 1992, after joining the competition at the last moment due to the disqualification of the Yugoslavian team, the Danish national football (soccer) team surprised themselves and the world when they won the European Championship. The nation erupted in celebration which lasted days and brought the whole country out of their homes to party in the streets. To some Danes, this moment placed Denmark on the map.

Danish Society

Political System

National Politics

The Danish parliament is called *Folketinget*. There are 179 members of parliament with 175 from Denmark, 2 from Greenland and 2 from the Faeroe Islands. Elections take place at least every four years, but usually occur at somewhat shorter intervals. To be eligible for a seat in *Folketinget*, you must be at least 18 years old, a Danish citizen and living in Denmark.

Private citizens have the right to vote at the age of 18. The parliament controls the governmental ministries and the legislative process.

Once *Folketinget* has passed a bill, the Queen's signature is required before it becomes law but this is just a technicality, her role is primarily ceremonial.

The Political Parties

A party must have at least 2% of the popular vote in order to have seats in *Folketinget*. *Folketinget* is currently made up of 10 political parties.

Right

Dansk Folkeparti (The Danish People's Party)
Fremskridtspartiet (The Progress Party)
Venstre* (The Left)
Det Konservative Folkeparti (The Conservative People's Party)

---

*Despite the name, this is actually one of Denmark's most conservative parties.

Center
Centrumdemokraterne (The Center Democrats)
Kristeligt Folkeparti (The Christian People's Party)
Det Radikale Venstre (The Social Liberal Party)

Left
Socialdemokratiet (The Social Democratic Party)
SF Socialistisk Folkeparti (The Socialist People's Party)
Enhedslisten (The Red-Green Alliance)

The Prime Minister (*statsministeren*) in Denmark is frequently elected from the largest party in the *Folketing*. However, cooperation and communication are essential elements of Danish politics since Danish governments usually have been minority governments. Usually Denmark has coalition governments so the parties will always try to find a candidate for Prime Minister from within the parties who meets the demands of all the coalition parties.

Local Government
Denmark is divided into 275 municipalities (*kommuner*) and 14 counties (*amter*). Every four years, local elections take place. Foreigners who have officially resided in Denmark for at least 3 years are entitled to vote in the municipal elections (*kommunalvalgene*).

At the municipal level, the local governments are responsible for social services such as schools, libraries, nurseries, daycare, public sports facilities and swimming pools, city buses, heating, electricity and water, and traffic signals. The county governments hold responsibility for the regional services such as hospitals and health insurance, busses, traffic, 'high schools' (*gymnasium*), adult assistance programs and some of the educational programs (including refugee centers).

The Welfare State

Denmark and the rest of Scandinavia often receive a great deal of attention for their social service systems. The Danish welfare model offers benefits to all citizens despite their employment or family situation. Recipients are considered individuals; each person receives his/her own share.

Danes are entitled to a wide variety of services. The ultimate goal of the system is to distribute the wealth of the nation so that no one is forced out of his/her home and onto the streets during difficult times. Thus, citizens have the right to free education, health care, retirement pension payments plus a wide variety of extra allowances depending on circumstances.

Below are a few examples of some of these extra allowances:

- women are entitled to up to 6 months maternity leave while men can also take 2 weeks in connection with the birth of a child and can, if they so desire, take some of their partner's maternity leave time;
- depending on income, some renters can get subsidies to help pay their rent;
- regardless of income level, mothers get a monetary allowance 4 times a year for each child in the house;
- the elderly can get free in-home help depending on income and circumstance;
- if necessary, the elderly can get money for heating;
- all handicapped citizens are entitled to any special equipment or facilities they may require.

This list goes on and on. In general, the Danish welfare model touches every aspect of life. Lately, it is becoming more and more difficult to accommodate all the needs of all the citizens. With rising medical costs and priorities, cutbacks are increasing. However, the Danes continue to be willing to pay very high personal income tax to maintain their welfare system.

Work Ethic

Training, education and practical experience make up the Danish worker. At all levels of society, Danes take great pride in their work. The employed often receive on-the-job training to upgrade their skills, while the unemployed are trained and retrained to allow them to get into the workforce. The average worker puts in 37 hours a week and gets 25 days of paid vacation plus legal holidays. The unions have been strong in keeping the workweek compact by mandating that retail shops close mid-day on Saturdays and all day Sunday. Only in the last 5-10 years have these hours become extended.

Since in most cases both parents work out of the house, family time can be the first thing to suffer. Therefore, in an attempt to spend 'quality time' with one's partner and/or child(ren), personal time is utilized to its fullest. Although many will choose to work overtime, few are willing to accept longer hours. In fact, in the spring of 1998 a general strike in which one of the demands was an extra week of paid vacation time took down the nation for over two weeks. In the end, workers in some fields gained a couple of days and some additional time for families with children.

In comparison with nations where 2 weeks of vacation is considered a luxury, the Danes obviously have nothing to complain about. However, this does show the determination of the people to keep their work time from overflowing into their personal time.

In conjunction with this respect for free time comes a slower pace of work life than in, for example, the United States or Japan. People seem to have a great deal of patience and are accepting of the fact that certain services take time. Since most visiting scholars and foreign students will be working and studying in state run institutions, you should be aware that things happen at their own pace. It will do you no good to complain or bang your head against a wall. Nothing is going to move any faster. Naturally, there are those who run around frantically and do the work of two people, but in general, the pace in the public sector is leisurely and people take their time. In recent years, however, much is done to combat bureaucratic arrogance. One interesting point in this regard is that over 800,000 Danes work in the public sector translating into almost one-quarter of the workforce. This has remained steady since the beginning of the 1980s.

The Law of Jante – Janteloven

With the desire for equality among the citizens of Denmark, the Danes live in the shadow of the Law of Jante (*Janteloven*). Created originally in 1933 by Danish/Norwegian author Aksel

The Law of Jante offers a satiric look at conformist values in Danish society. From early years children are taught to honor collaboration over competition. Show-offs and flashy attitudes are frowned on.

Sandemose, *Janteloven* offers a satiric look at conformist values which have come to be associated with Nordic cultures, specifically Danish culture. The 'law' basically says that one should not put him/herself above the next person.

Janteloven epitomizes the negative values of a group mentality and has become a metaphor for group thinking that discourages individualism and individual achievement. In reality, the concept of *Janteloven* is intertwined in the fabric of Danish society. From early years children are taught to honor collaboration over competition. The education system teaches to the middle of the class and encourages group work and cooperative learning. The social systems of the state stress the right to be taken care of by the group, regardless of social status. No one is better than the next guy. This translates into a nation of people who strive to communicate across social classes, with relatively little homelessness or poverty and little extreme wealth – basically the general population is comfortable. Thus, show-offs and flashy attitudes are frowned on in Denmark. You will not see many decadent displays of wealth or power. On the contrary, the rich and famous are expected to wait in line like anybody else.

The Role of Women

Perhaps the best place to start when considering the role of women in Danish society is with the general concept of sexuality in the country. Sexuality in this society is healthy and relaxed with fewer 'rules' than some other cultures. Naturally, every society has stereotypical dominating men and coquettish women, but in Denmark these qualities are not necessarily the norm. Men and women interact with one another on an equal playing field and in doing so eliminate some of the tension found between the sexes in other countries. The general public pays little attention to stories of politicians' personal lives or even office gossip. Professional reputations are not destroyed on the basis of personal relationships. Stemming from this relaxed atmosphere, public nudity on beaches and in parks is openly allowed and accepted, as is nudity in newspapers, advertising and on television.

This sexual liberation in Denmark appears to lead to a sense of equality for women in the country. Unwed motherhood, cohabitation outside of marriage and divorce are not uncommon in Danish society. Women have a variety of lifestyle choices that may not be possible in other countries.

Education also reflects the process of creating equality between the sexes. In Denmark, the ratio of men to women enrolled in higher education programs in the 1990s has reached 1:1. This provides positive opportunities for the future. However, the issue of child rearing continues to impact opportunities for women in the workplace. The state has tried to equalize this by providing adequate daycare facilities for children and paternity leave for new fathers.

The Church

The Reformation of the 1500s brought Protestantism to Denmark. During this time King Christian III took the opportunity to seize dominance from the Catholic Church and forced Catholic bishops to give up their power over the people by imprisoning them and confiscating their land. Denmark became a nation of Protestants. However, it took 300 years to establish freedom of religion in the country (1849, *Grundlov*).

Protestantism remains the prevailing religion in the country today. In 1997, 86% of the population was listed as members of the Evangelical Lutheran Church – the Church of Denmark (*Folkekirken*). The remaining 14% of the population belong to various other Christian and non-Christian churches. The Jewish community, established in 1814 and made up of approximately 3400 members, is the oldest non-Christian community in Denmark. More recently, the Muslim community established itself in the country through immigration. There are currently approximately 84,000 members of separate Islamic communities.

Today, only a small percentage of the population actually go to church services on a regular basis. Many Danes utilize the church for the special occasions in their lives including baptisms, confirmations, weddings and funerals. The Church tries to maintain a contemporary perspective and mirror the trends of Danish society. Therefore, it is not uncommon to find female pastors as leaders of the religious community.

The Arts

Art in all forms is a part of Danish society: Music, dance, film, painting, sculpture, design, architecture –the list goes on and on. Each year, a part of the national budget is reserved for special individuals who have given a great deal to the nation. These artists are rewarded with a lifetime Civil List pension. Others have the opportunity to apply for annual funds to help them with the expenses of their craft.

Queen Margrethe II is a major supporter of the arts and is herself an internationally recognized designer and painter. Other renown 20th century Danes include Karen Blixen (Isak Dinesen) (author), Jørgen Utzon (architect), Victor Borge (entertainer and pianist), Peter Høeg (author), Lars von Trier (film director), and Jørgen Nash (painter).

Higher Education

Studenter

Each year in June, all across Denmark, the graduating secondary school students don white caps and make their way from party to party in celebration of the end of their studies. This celebration is, however, twofold. First of all, these students have just completed what is known as their *studentereksamen* (Upper Secondary School Leaving Examination) and second, they now qualify for admission to a university or other institution of higher education.

Each year in June, the graduating secondary school students don white caps.

The students attended high school, better known in Denmark as *gymnasium* for three years of rigorous academic preparation. The *gymnasium* curricula, in contrast to Danish vocational secondary school programs, provides students with a general education as well as the academic skills necessary for continuing their studies. The *gymnasium* curriculum is offered in two lines – languages and mathematics – which share a common core of obligatory subjects. To graduate, all students must pass a total of ten subject examinations, including a written examination in Danish language and literature and two exams in at least two subjects that have been studied at the advanced level. Due to the stringent examinations and curricula at the secondary school level, Danish *gymnasium* graduates have been compared to students completing their freshman year in, for example, an American university. The average age of the *gymnasium* graduate is 19, which also makes them a bit older than their North American, Southern European and Asian counterparts.

Higher Education – Admission Requirements

With the passing of *studentereksamen* or its adult education equivalent, the Higher Preparatory Examination (HF), Danish students have earned the right to attend the wide variety of institutions of higher education. All applicants with these qualifications can find a place at one of the more than 130 Danish institutions of higher education. Best of all, there is no tuition charge for those who qualify as higher education is subsidized by the Danish government. However, higher education is no free ride. The Danish students and their parents have been paying for this privilege for years – through their high taxes.

In order to accommodate all those who wish to attend college or university, a quota system has been established. The places in Quota I are for those students with a Danish qualifying examination. Quota II provides slots for those applicants who meet admission requirements of particular schools or programs by more traditional means: a period of relevant employment, prolonged travel abroad or foreign educational qualifications. It is through Quota II that international students can enroll in regular Danish study programs. All applications are evaluated individually by each institution.

In general, students without Danish qualifying examinations applying for degree programs in Danish institutions of higher education must meet all the same requirements as their Danish counterparts, including proving proficiency in the Danish language at an advanced level. However, recently, in an effort to internationalize and attract more students from abroad, more and more Danish universities and colleges offer special degree programs where the language of instruction is English. Note that international students coming to Denmark will find themselves competing with the Danes for places in these programs, which are increasingly popular and competitive.

Below is a list of examples of accepted qualifications for admission to a Danish college or university:

- upper secondary certificates and diplomas from the Nordic countries, European Union countries and other countries that have signed the European Convention on the Equivalence of Diplomas Leading to Admission to Universities;
- the International and the European Baccalaureate;
- high school diplomas from the United States either followed by up to two years of university or college studies in relevant subjects or supplemented by three advanced placement examinations in relevant subjects with a grade of 3 or higher. This also applies to applicants with a high school diploma from countries with a similar educational system (e.g., Japan);
- and bachelor's degrees in relevant subjects from universities in Bangladesh, India, Pakistan and the Philippines.

Each individual institution decides on admission. Further information about entrance qualifications and supplementary tests can be obtained from the admission offices at the institutions.

Colleges and Universities

Opportunities in the Danish higher educational system are quite varied. The institutions are divided into two classifications – colleges and universities. The college classification is generally made up of more than 100 small, specialized institutions with 400-600 students each. Programs in the college classification are usually shorter than those at the university, offering professionally oriented training in areas such as social work, physiotherapy, teacher training, nursing, engineering, design, music and other disciplines.

The university classification includes five multi-disciplinary universities, ten institutions specializing in such fields as engineering, pharmacy, art, architecture, veterinary science, agriculture and business studies, and six music academies. Danish universities offer courses and carry out research in traditional academic fields.

Changes over the past 10 years in the higher education system have resulted in a university system that is closer to the Anglo-Saxon system than the previous 4-6 years of specialized study before any degree was granted. Usually students select a major field of study before they start their coursework. Students then follow a 3-4 year course leading to a bachelor's degree followed by 2 years of study for a master's degree (*candidatus* degree). Three additional years of study and supervised research (including approximately 6 months of coursework) along with an oral defense of a written dissertation, are required to earn a Ph.D. The defense is an open public lecture where the Ph.D. candidate presents his/her work and is challenged by a team of two or three senior researchers in the field.

In recent years there has been a great deal of interest in expanding Ph.D. programs in Danish universities. To develop internationally minded researchers, many Ph.D. students are encouraged to spend at least one semester abroad. To enhance their global perspective, Ph.D. students are required to participate in at least two active research groups or networks (preferably international). This provides the opportunities for these junior researchers to develop professional ties and present their research. Lastly, Ph.D. students are required to teach for a specified number of hours.

Ph.D. holders who fulfill an additional 5-8 years of original and demanding research may be awarded the traditional Danish post-doctoral degree (dr. phil, dr. merc., dr. scient. etc). Note that this degree can also be awarded to researchers who do not have a Ph.D.

Course credits and grading scale

When attempting to understand the value of a grading scale of another school, it is important not to automatically assume that the practice of grading is similar to your own. In a country like the United States, for instance, grading scales can differ greatly from one state to the next, or from one school to the next for that matter, since there is no official regulation for distributing academic grades. In Denmark, however, where education at all levels, including higher education, is regulated by the Ministry of Education, the grading scale and its use is described in a ministerial order. In addition, in order to maintain stability and fight grade inflation or local interpretation of exams, external examiners from universities and colleges across the country participate in almost all higher educational exams.

Thus all schools in Denmark utilize the same 13 point grading scale. The grades break down as follows:

10-13	excellent performance
7-9	average to good performance
6	acceptable performance
00-5	poor or unacceptable performance.

Some exams are graded on a pass/fail basis. Students must receive a grade of at least 6 to pass.

A grade of 13 is rarely awarded and is only given out in exceptional cases. Therefore, when comparing grade-point-averages, Danish grades should not necessarily be compared with other systems in regard to top grades. Although the grading system is not based on a curve, the awarding of grades tends to fall in line with a normal distribution. Table 1 below shows the grades earned in all exams taken at the Copenhagen Business School's Faulty of Economics and Business Administration in 1997. As you can see, less than 1% of those taking exams at both the undergraduate and graduate levels received a grade of 13.

Table 1. Copenhagen Business School, Faculty of Economics and Business Administration, 1997

Grade	Number of exams (undergraduate)	%	Number of exams (graduate)	%
13	53	0.40	97	0.95
11	470	3.20	587	5.77
10	1470	9.90	1331	13.09
9	2242	15.10	1896	18.65
8	2700	18.20	2068	20.34
7	2487	16.80	1528	15.03
6	2080	14.00	1168	11.49
5	1770	11.90	852	8.38
03	1200	8.10	315	3.10
00	352	2.40	323	3.18
Total	14,824	100.00	10,165	100.00
Average grade	7.06		7.63	

Danish students are not officially tested quite as often as students in some countries, but the exams they take are comprehensive in nature and quite challenging. In general, exams tend to be essay format where the students are expected to write for approximately 4-6 hours. Written projects, prepared individually or in groups, may be followed by an oral examination. In addition, oral examinations are also common without a preceding paper.

Since 1993, all incoming students are required to take exams after their first year of study. There are a variety of models but students who do not receive a grade of at least 6 on each of these exams may not be permitted to continue their studies. These exams are generally offered in June, with make-up and re-exams in August. Students have 3 chances to pass these exams. In addition, before graduation, students must pass a number or oral and written exams. It is, however, becoming increasingly normal for exams to be held at the end of each semester, in January and May/June. Since academic calendars from country to country can differ, it is vital that international students confirm the dates of their exams prior to making any travel plans. Exam dates are often posted on bulletin boards in your department.

Educational Administration

Since universities in Denmark are all public and fall under the same government act (from 1993), the administrative hierarchies of these institutions are the same and function in a very democratic fashion. All members of higher education, including teacher-researchers, administrative staff and students, have a voice in this system.

What is worth emphasizing here is that the students in Denmark have a very strong voice and actively participate in curricular reform. Student representatives work to protect the interests of the students at all levels of higher education.

For detailed information regarding the management of higher education in Denmark consult The University Act, 1993, available from the Ministry of Education or the Danish Rectors' Conference.

Social Life at Danish Universities

Campus Life

Danish colleges and universities are usually made up of departmental units and administrative offices, a library system, cafeteria(s) and sometimes a café or two thrown in for good measure. Students attending Danish institutions of higher education do not expect more of the campus. What this means is that the Danish campus consists of what in other countries might be considered a bare-bones structure. In general, you will not find athletic facilities, health centers, or housing offices on Danish college campuses. Danish students and visiting scholars need to look beyond the college campus for extra-curricular activities such as intramural sports, orchestras or choirs. This also means that you will not find school mascots, sports teams or school songs.

As in other countries, university life in Denmark can be the center of a student's social world. Students tend to get to know each other through casual get-togethers in their respective academic departments and divisions. Many schools have a variety of political and non-political formal student organizations which arrange social functions for the student body. In most cases, these parties have a cover charge of a minimal fee and some type of enticing theme to draw you in. Often, the International Office of a college or university will also arrange regularly scheduled functions such as parties, films or outings to provide a venue for Danish and international students to mix and mingle. In addition, many schools will have international clubs where students and faculty meet for casual language exchange and just to make new friends and acquaintances.

Although there is this sense of school spirit, both studying and working in a Danish university setting are viewed much like full-time jobs. Much of what goes on in a university happens between the hours of 8 a.m. and 5 p.m. There are evening classes at many schools that include some regular courses, Open University courses and continuing education programs. Only recently have university libraries begun to expand their opening hours to include Saturdays and Sundays to allow students to research and study outside of regular working hours.

In general, professors and researchers work a standard 12-month cycle with an average workweek of 37 hours. For a full-time, tenure-track position this means 37 hours divided up between teaching, research and committee work. Faculty members do not have summers 'off'. Like all Danes, faculty members are entitled to five weeks vacation annually of which three can be consecutive. However, unlike in many other countries, professors are expected to report to work all year round. Since there is little tradition for summer schools in Denmark, university life for a researchers is a bit looser during the summer months and they are generally free to conduct their research where they see fit.

You may notice that interpersonal relationships appear somewhat casual at Danish institutions. From the start, administrative, academic and student groups will strive to achieve a sense of warmth/comfort (*hygge*) within departments. Orientation programs for incoming students help to build rapport through intensive group-building activities and functions. So, although Danish institutions of higher education do not provide a great number of extra-curricular activities throughout the academic year, students develop a sense of belonging and school ownership and often find themselves utilizing the school's facilities for social functions. Thus, on a Friday afternoon you can expect to find a room full of students in the cafeteria or café mingling over beer and sodas enjoying their institution's facilities. This is referred to as *'fredagsbar'* (Friday's bar).

Students have little patience for lectures that they do not feel are worthwhile and often choose absenteeism as a viable option.

As you might expect, university life for students in Denmark is a series of appointments, classes and projects. Although lectures and courses are considered important, Danish students, in comparison to their counterparts in other nations, do not tend to consider class participation, as vital to their academic success as, for example, research or exam preparation. Students receive no grade for participation and can often gather notes from their classmates or professors. Since there are few tests or quizzes to worry about, most students focus on the long-term projects required by their degree programs, their comprehensive examinations and their final theses. Students have little patience for classes and lectures that they do not feel are worthwhile and often choose absenteeism as a viable option. Instead, they may choose to work independently on individual and group projects with the goal of completing their degree requirements.

This independent spirit is a strong characteristic among Danish students. Colleges and universities do not function *in loco parentis*. In contrast to students from other nations, the

Danish students do not rely heavily on their parents for support during their college years. With tuition and living expenses covered at least to a basic degree by government grants, Danish students often choose to live on their own in apartments or dormitories and run their lives very independently of their families. Also, it is very common for Danish students to take on part time jobs where some work up to twenty hours a week to earn extra money.

In addition to the financial end of things, much of the decision making in higher education takes care of itself when it comes to life at college. For most students, the question of what to study was answered back in high school or post-secondary school programs based of which program they participated in. The application process then guides students toward a course of study. As undergraduates, students begin a program that is, in general, within one area of specialization. There is of course room for elective courses, personal interest and further specialization in later graduate study.

Danes On the Move

You will find that Danes at colleges and universities are quite well traveled and knowledgeable about geography and foreign cultures. Many students participate in study abroad programs during their secondary school years to get a head start. In general, Danes try to take advantage of affordable charter tour prices and make their way to all ends of the earth. Often, some choose to take a year of travel after graduating from high school before entering college. Some simply travel for recreation, others take part in internships and au pair programs abroad to improve their foreign language skills. This is another reason why Danish first-year college students tend to be a bit older and more mature than their international counterparts. The students bring their experience and independence to the classroom and to their studies.

In general, the government takes care of basic educational

and living expenses; thus Danish students are not reliant on their families for support. The same holds true for outgoing exchange students. In most cases, exchange places can be offered to the students at little personal expense. This allows students of limited means to also participate in study abroad exchange programs. Although the funding covers only the bare necessities, its mere existence provides the incentive to study abroad for a student who might otherwise not be able to afford this luxury. This independence from family financial support creates a much different atmosphere than in nations where higher education is tuition driven. Of course, the Danes do want to have fun abroad and this is where the part-time jobs come in handy.

Danish institutions of higher education participate widely in a variety of international partnerships. As a result of the EU, Danes actively exchange students through programs such as ERASMUS, COMETT, SOCRATES and LEONARDO. Beyond the European borders the Danes have established numerous exchange programs in the Americas and more recently in Asia. Denmark's educational borders are stretching with greater numbers of students and professors taking advantage of these new liaisons. In addition to sending Danes abroad, there have been concerted efforts to bring more students and researchers into Denmark.

Thus, Danish students have a wide variety of exchange programs available to them. Each institution works to arrange exchange places for Danish students in institutions outside Denmark with the desire that a certain percentage of their student population participate in a study abroad program for at least one semester during their higher education. Since the level of academic English skills achieved by a large percentage of Danes attending colleges and universities is quite strong, Danish students tend to blend easily into foreign institutions where the language of instruction is English.

Of course, study abroad is not limited to exchange programs. Some students will choose to study abroad in pursuit of a foreign degree or as special students at a foreign university.

These students are known as 'free movers'. This is a more expensive option than an exchange semester. Although the Danish government basically covers general expenses, free movers are responsible for all tuition fees at foreign universities. Thus, exchange programs remain a more popular choice of study abroad option. Table 2 illustrates the rise in student movement to and from Denmark.

Table 2.

Total students to and from Denmark*			
Year	Total	Outgoing Students	Incoming Students
1995/96	5668	3384	2284
1996/97	6167	3588	2579
1997/98	6748	3818	2930

Source: Danish Rectors' Conference 1999.

*) This calculation includes the total number of students at tertiary education institutions under the Danish Ministry of Education involved in student mobility over 3 months. The calculation is based on reports submitted by the institutions.

Over the past few years, the internationalization efforts in Danish higher education have been on the rise. In 1997, the Danish Rectors' Conference published a small booklet on the debate surrounding these efforts. In this booklet they call on the institutions of higher education to bear in mind that internationalization is not a single concept that can be separated from other strategy plans of a college or university. On the contrary, the process must become part of the overall scheme of each institution. In a small country like Denmark, the process of internationalization is crucial in ensuring Danish society and the business community globally competitive graduates. This process therefore includes not just sending and receiving students, but researchers and lecturers as well. Ph.D. programs in Denmark make a focused effort to provide opportunities for junior researchers to train in other countries.

International Students in Denmark

Each year students from all over the world come to Denmark to take advantage of the academic opportunities the institutions of higher education have to offer. Some come for only a semester, while others stay for years. The differences between coming to Denmark as an exchange student versus as a degree student can effect the experience one has while studying abroad.

For those students coming to Denmark for study exchange programs, the legwork begins at home. The universities and colleges in Denmark have a vast network of exchange places set up with schools all around the world. This means that a school in Canada, for example, sends a Canadian student to the University of Aarhus and in exchange accepts one Danish student for a specific period of study. In general exchange places are available for one to two semesters and offer students a chance to get a feel for life in a different country, culture and academic environment.

Although Danish is the national language of Denmark, English is slowly gaining ground in institutions of higher education. School children in Denmark begin learning foreign languages, in particular English and German, between the ages of 8-12. This leads to a very high proficiency in languages in Denmark in general and in Danish higher education in particular. Because of this, students proficient in English who wish to come to Denmark on exchange programs do not need to have any background in the Danish language. English has become the standard language for courses offered to exchange students to Denmark.

In determining which courses to choose, exchange students should take the time to carefully read catalogues and make sure that the courses available are suitable for credit transfer back to the home university. Since the courses available to international students must be offered in languages other than Danish (usually English), the choices can be somewhat limited in comparison to the options available to the Danish students. Be aware that no matter what school you choose, your first choice of course may not always be available for a variety of reasons.

Courses can become over-enrolled, can be canceled, can overlap in terms of time of day they are offered or you may simply not be interested in the topic once you have attended the course. The best advice for all students is to be prepared to change course selection if the need arises and have a list of alternative course choices on hand.

It is vital that issues regarding credit transfer, course options, financial responsibility and language proficiency are clarified prior to arrival in Denmark. Establishing links with the appropriate administrative staff and advisors at both your home university and in Denmark can make all the difference in terms of a successful exchange program experience. The Danish college or university will have an international office and student advisors who will assist you in registering for courses and finding your way around in a new environment, but they do not have the access to or knowledge of all the administrative systems at your home university.

Those coming to Denmark to pursue degree programs need to consider other issues. According to the Danish Rectors' Conference, non-Danish students looking to complete a degree from a Danish college or university must prove that they have sufficient command of Danish and hold with a Danish qualifying examination or qualifications recognized or assessed as equivalent. With a push toward internationalization, more and more institutions are beginning to offer degree programs where the language of instruction and examination is English. Danish proficiency is not required for such programs. For more information, contact the school of your choice directly.

No matter whether you are an exchange student or a full-time degree student, you will inevitably find certain cultural difference from your home university or college to that of your Danish institution. Just as there are cultural differences in food and dress, cultural differences exists in terms of educational norms, expectations and traditions in Danish institutions of higher education. Obviously, where you come from will determine how different it is in Denmark from what you are accustomed to but the following are a few areas to be aware of as you prepare to study in a new environment.

As mentioned above, relationships between professors and students may feel much more relaxed than what you are normally accustomed to. In Denmark, students customarily call their professors by their first name and drop the formality of titles such as professor or doctor. This first-name intimacy alleviates much of the formality of the classroom and allows students the freedom to discuss a wide variety of issues without formal constraints. Professors are not considered the keepers of knowledge; instead they represent a source from which to gain knowledge and information. This philosophy leads to an atmosphere of student responsibility. A great deal of the course work in Danish universities and colleges require independent initiative on the part of the student in order to complete most assignments and group projects.

For students coming to Denmark from cultures where classes are all teacher fronted and the professor has the last word, Denmark may present a change. Students are expected to actively participate in classes and voice their opinions if they

For students coming from cultures where classes are all teacher fronted and the professor has the last word, Denmark may present a change.

disagree with a professor's opinion or analysis (that is if they have something constructive to say!). The Danish classroom offers a venue to express thoughts, experiment with ideas and challenge theories. Some international students feel that the required work in their Danish courses is not as strenuous as at their home university because the professors do not assign what they consider very tough assignments. In reality, Danish professors put the onus on the students to develop an assignment by going beyond the reading list, the homework assignment or the course discussion. In addition to attending lectures and seminars, Danish students are expected to establish study groups and complete independent research. Much of the coursework in Danish degree programs is meant to lay the foundation for the students' exams and ultimately for the bachelor- and master's theses. As noted above, preparing for examinations at the Danish university requires in depth reading on a broad scale and, as any Danish student will tell you, the exams are challenging.

Practical Matters

Visas

All visitors to Denmark must have a valid passport to enter the country. Visa requirements to enter the country vary and are always subject to change, so it is always wise to check with the Danish embassy or consultant in your area before finalizing any travel plans. In general, other than citizens of other Scandinavian countries, students who study in Denmark must obtain a residency permit. Visiting academic staff and foreign researchers and employees are required to get a resident/work permit. Note that you may risk being sent out of the country if you enter on false premises, e.g. a tourist visa.

For citizens of other EU countries, the paperwork is relatively straightforward. EU nationals can enter the country and stay in Denmark for up to 3 months without any special paperwork. If you plan to stay for more than 3 months, you must have a residence permit. It is not necessary to apply for a residence permit prior to your arrival in Denmark, but shortly after you arrive you must go to your local municipality (*kommune*) office to get your permit. The institution where you will study or work should provide you with the appropriate paperwork to take with you to the *kommune* office. To get the permit, you will need: 1) passport or EU identity card; 2) two passport-size pictures; and 3) the paperwork from your institution.

Non-European citizens are required to get their residence and work permits prior to landing in Denmark. This means that plans must be made well enough in advance to allow for the handling of paperwork (approximately 6-10 weeks). Once your position as a visiting student or scholar has been secured, you will receive the appropriate papers from your institution.

After filling out the necessary information, you should send/take the papers and two passport-size photos to the nearest Danish embassy or consulate for processing. Included in your paperwork to be sent to the embassy should be a light-purple form that you will receive from your host institution. Do NOT send this back to your host institution but directly to the embassy with your visa application. You should be prepared to produce proof that you are able to finance your stay abroad.

Nordic citizens need to bring an Internordic Certificate of Change of Address *(Internordisk flyttebevis)* which can be obtained from your local authorities *(kommunekontoret)*.

Student Work Permits

The principle rule is that students from Scandinavian countries and from other EU member states usually do not need a work permit for normal student jobs for a limited period of time. Check with the Danish Immigration Service *(udlændingestyrelsen)* for more information.

Students from all other countries can only undertake paid employment if they have a work permit. An application for a work permit must be submitted to the Danish embassy in the home country prior to leaving for Denmark. The unemployment rate in Denmark means that the chances of finding a job are very small, which is why international students should not base their economic standing on the chance of getting paid employment – full or part time.

Civil Registration Number (CPR number)

A civil registration number (*CPR* number – birth date plus 4 digits) is issued at the Civil Registrar's Office *(Folkeregisteret)* in the area in which you reside. The CPR number is used in connection with all public social services offered at institutions such as clinics, hospitals, libraries, banks, etc. Thus, it is impor-

Civil Registration Number (CPR number)

tant to get to the *Folkeregister* as soon as possible after you have received your residence permit/work permit. The international office or welcome center at your university of college should be able to direct you to the nearest office in your municipality. You will need to bring your passport with you to the *Folkeregister*. The CPR number will be sent to you in a 4-6 weeks.

Health Insurance

When you go to the *Folkeregister* to get your CPR number (see above), you will be asked to choose a physician from a list of medical doctors in your area. After a six-week qualifying period, you will be issued a yellow, plastic medical insurance card (*sygesikringsbevis*). This card will have your name, address, CPR number and name and address of your physician.

Since the Danish national health system services are not available to new residents for six weeks, you need to make certain that you have some type of private health insurance cover-

Although a vist to the doctor as well as any hospitalization are free of charge, dental and optical work are not covered by the Danish system.

age to cover this period of time. When you enter the country, you may be asked to present documentation of such coverage.

Nordic citizens are covered from the start by the Danish national health system and will get hospital services free of charge according to the Nordic Convention.

For EU citizens, the least complicated solution is to get an E-111 form from your local health office. Upon application, this form provides you with 3 months of medical coverage in the specified EU country.

Under the Danish system, visits to the doctor, as well as any hospitalization, are free of charge. However, dental and optical work are not covered. In addition, payment for prescriptions, eye glasses or contact lenses are your own responsibility.

One more note of caution in regard to travel insurance. Although you are covered by the Danish national health system six weeks after you register with the *Folkeregister*, the system does not cover the costs of medical repatriation. This would be necessary if, for example, you were involved in an accident and wanted to spend a period of prolonged recovery at home. Expenses of this sort can be disastrous for an individual or their family. To be safe, make sure that you take out all the necessary travel insurance policies prior to leaving your home country.

Medication

Usually, no special immunizations are required or recommended before entry into Denmark.

Prescriptions from other countries are not generally accepted in Denmark, although occasionally they can be re-prescribed by your local Danish doctor. Be aware that the names of pharmaceutical products vary from country to country. To avoid any possible difficulties, bring a supply of any prescription medications you will need for the period you are in Denmark. In addition, it is always wise to have a doctor's written prescription or note with you in order to permit smooth customs inspection and to show a local Danish doctor in case you run short.

Money and Banking

Currency

You will see three different abbreviations for the Danish crown (*krone*) – DKK in the international money markets, Dkr in most of northern Europe, and most often kr. in Denmark. One *krone* can be divided into 100 *øre*. Coins in the following denominations are in circulation: 25 *øre*, 50 *øre*, 1 *krone*, 2 *kroner*, 5 *kroner*, 10 *kroner* and 20 *kroner*. Notes come in denominations of 50, 100, 200, 500 and 1000 *kroner*.

To give you an idea of what to expect, the following currencies convert at these approximate rates (as of January 1999):

Currency	DKK/unit	unit/DKK
British Pounds £	10.68	0.0936
European Monetary Union €	7.437	0.1354
Japanese Yen ¥	0.05436	17.85
United States Dollar $	6.479	0.1543

Up to date exchange rates and currency conversion programs can be found on the Internet. One convenient address is www.xe.net/currency/.

Changing money in Denmark is not difficult as most Danish banks will convert a wide range of currencies (notes, not coins) and traveler's checks but it can be expensive. Make sure to ask about both the exchange rates and fees and commissions. Danish banks charge large fees for cashing travelers checks and bank notes (even those in *kroner*).

One suggestion to avoid hefty charges is to use debit, credit and cash cards. For those staying only a few months, you can take money directly out of your savings, checking or credit card accounts from you home bank with minimal charges for each transaction. Money can be drawn from selected banks and automatic teller machines (ATMs). Most ATMs work the same way as in your home country. You will need to have a personal identification number (PIN) to access your accounts. Be sure to ask your bank to explain all the conditions for using this type of banking.

If you plan to stay in Denmark for more than one semester, it is wise to open a local bank account. In most cases, you will need to have your CPR number before you can get a bank account. Some colleges and universities will have agreements with specific banks where you can open an account right away. In this situation, the school will provide you with a letter that you can present to the bank.

A great deal of Danish money handling is conducted electronically. Many people utilize a debit card know as a DANKORT for most of their daily purchases. A DANKORT can be a major asset since it can be used all across the country for almost any type of purchase. In addition, you can draw cash out from your account when you make a purchase at a local shop. DANKORT cards which double as VISA/Master Card cards are also available. A VISA/MC DANKORT will allow you to access your money internationally through any ATM or bank.

In addition to the DANKORT card, a new plastic card is being promoted which works much like a telephone card and can be used in a variety of shops in place of cash. 100 kr. and 200 kr DANMØNT cards can be purchased at some banks, train stations and kiosks. The hope is that the popularity of this card will increase, reducing the need for currency.

Tipping

Taxi fares and restaurant bills include service charges in their prices. Therefore, you are not expected to add extra to the total. Tipping is becoming more customary when service has been particularly good. In these instances, 10-15% of the pre-tax total is more than adequate.

Weather

The normal average temperature for Copenhagen is 2.2°C/36°F in February, 15°C/59°F in May, 20°C/68°F in August and 7°C/44.6°F in November. Although temperatures seldom drop below freezing in the winter, wind chill, high levels of humidity and limited hours of daylight can make it feel much colder than it actually is. Although the winters can be cold and dark,

In general, people do not come to Denmark for the weather. When the sun is shining, however, people tend to drop everything they are doing.

with an average of 7 hours of daylight in December, the summers are mild and bright. The longest days of the year are in late June, when the suns rises around 4:30 am and sets around 10:00 pm.
In general, people do not come to Denmark for the weather. On a whole, you can expect gray skies, wind and rain. However, when the sun is shining the entire Danish population takes note. Do not be surprised if people drop everything they are doing to enjoy a bright sunny day. In the summer months you will find people spread out in every park and cafe taking in the sun's rays during the day and the long twilight skies in the evening.

Shopping

When it comes to shopping, the Danes are committed to quality. People tend to prefer to buy the best they can afford for their homes, their wardrobes and their pantries. Fresh food is at the center of Danish life, which means that people shop more frequently for small amounts of groceries each time. Large supermarket chains are very common across the country as well as small stall and markets in the larger cities. Although prices for food in Denmark can seem overwhelming, do not despair. In addition to the specialty food shops and high end shops there are also discount shops and supermarkets. Below is a list of some of the more common stores found across the country. (Bear in mind, value added tax – VAT – is 25% in Denmark.)

Discount Supermarket	**Standard Supermarket**
(minimal customer service and selection)	*(including specialty items and home supplies)*
Aldi	Kvickly
Netto	Føtex
Fakta	Superbrugsen
	Irma

Some useful vocabulary when shopping for food:

Meat	**Kød**
beef	oksekød
chicken	kylling
ground beef	hakket oksekød
pork	svinekød
sausage/hot dog	pølse
turkey	kalkun
veal	kalvekød
Dairy Products	**Mejeriprodukter**
skim (no fat)	skummetmælk
low fat	letmælk
whole (full fat)	sødmælk
cream (for coffee)	kaffefløde
whipping cream	piskefløde

cheese	ost
butter	smør
sour cream	crème fraiche

Drinks	**Drikkevarer**
soft drinks	sodavand
mineral water	danskvand
beer	øl
coffee	kaffe
tea	te

Miscellaneous	**Diverse**
flour	mel
egg	æg
soap (hand)	sæbe
dishwashing liquid	opvaskemiddel
laundry detergent	vaskepulver
fruit	frugt
vegetables	grøntsager
organic products	økologiske varer

Recycling Bottles: When buying soft drinks or beer, you will usually pay a deposit of 1.25 kr. or 1.50 kr. deposit for small bottles, 2.50 kr. for liter bottles, and 4 kr. for 1 liter bottles. When you return the bottles, your deposit will be refunded.

General Shopping Hours
Most of the larger grocery stores are open from 9:00 am to 8:00 pm on weekdays and from 9:00-5:00 on Saturdays. In some of the smaller cities and town, the shops will close on the weekdays between 5:30 and 6:00 pm and around 2:00 pm on Saturdays. In general, the majority of shops are closed all day Sunday. On Sundays and legal holidays, bakeries, flower shops and kiosks (small convenience shops) are open part of the day.

Driving and Transportation

Driver's License

Driving in Denmark is considered a luxury activity. As such, obtaining a driver's license can be expensive. To begin with, driver's education classes are extremely costly. The regulations for driving in Denmark are strictly enforced and one must pass a stringent exam before being issued a license (240 kr.). But once attained, a Danish driver's license is good throughout the European Union countries and Scandinavia and is valid until the driver's 70th birthday.

On a more positive note, the Danish authorities will honor a visitor's national driver's license. For the first three months that you are in Denmark you are considered a tourist and can drive with your own driver's license as long as the writing on the license is written in a European language. If the license is written in a non-European language, you will need to also have an international driver's license.

After you establish residence, you are required to trade your license in for a Danish license. The charge for this service is 350 kr. If you hold a non-EU license, to get a license you will need to get a form from your doctor (see above) which states that you are fit to drive.

The doctor's office will charge 350 kr. for this service. Take this form, a passport picture, your driver's license and your passport (with your resident permit stamp) to your local police station to apply to a Danish driver's license.

The police will take your old license from you and issue you a temporary certificate. Your new license will be mailed to you in 2-4 weeks.

Automobile Registration

If you are brining a car into Denmark from another country, you must have the national sticker of the country where the vehicle is registered on the car. You can buy one of these at most service stations.

When you arrive, first contact the police in your area to get an automobile registration form (form P216E). On this form you must list details about the car and the owner. Usually, you can continue to drive your car with your foreign license plates for up to a year before you must have Danish plates. Next, you must contact the customs and tax office (*told- og skatteregioner*) to find out about taxes on your car. Cars registered in another EU country may be imported free of duty and VAT.

You may want to contact these offices prior to actually bringing a used car into the country. You may find that the cost of having a car in Denmark higher than you expect. Registration costs are calculated based on an estimate of the car's value. The fee is 180% of the car's value in Denmark (not in your home country – it does not matter what you paid for it at home 3 years ago!). Inspection costs run around 350 kr. and the license plate is 1040 kr.

The same registration fees and inspection costs hold true for vehicles purchased in Denmark. Be warned, having a car in Denmark is not cheap.

Transportation
Public transportation in Denmark is extensive, reliable and efficient. Tickets for buses and trains are interchangeable, making transfers hassle free. For example, in greater Copenhagen, a ticket can be used on any form of transportation. You buy an hour's access to the system. A basic ticket for one zone within the city is 11 kr., and the time you get on the bus or train is stamped on your ticket. For the hour your ticket is valid, you can use any bus or train in a city's system, as many times as you want. You can go back and forth on the same ticket for example, switch from bus to train, chain lines, etc. Note that 10-ride tickets (for a variety of different zone combinations) and especially monthly cards can reduce fares substantially.

Taxes

Part of the Danish experience is paying taxes. Due to the complexity of the tax laws and the high level of taxation, Danes are always on the lookout for new rules and regulation, especially ones that allow them to save a few *kroner*.

Once you have established residency, you are immediately subject to full taxation on all worldwide income the same as any other Dane. Each individual person (including children) in Denmark is treated as a separate taxpayer although there are some tax incentives for couples.

All personal income is taxable. Income after deductions is subject to a national income tax, two municipality taxes, and a voluntary church tax. There is also a national Labor Market Contribution.

Tax	%
1. National Tax	
Lower tax	8%
Middle tax	6%
(income in excess of DKK 139,000 (single) or DKK 278,000 (couple))	
Top tax	15%
(personal income plus positive net income exceeding DKK 251,200)	
2. Municipality Tax	26 – 34 %
3. Church Tax	0.4 – 1.5% (automatic voluntary tax)
4. Labor Market Contribution	8% (of gross income)

As you can see, most Danes end up paying at least 50% of their marginal income to the government. Although this seems like a huge bite out of take-home pay, there is a positive side to the high level of taxation. There are many services available to tax payers including pensions, healthcare and safe, clean streets, not to mention free education.

It is important for you to check with your host institution's personnel office to find out the specific details of your contract, salary and tax liability before you begin working in Denmark. In the taxation laws there are some tax exceptions for international researchers abroad as well as teachers from a number of countries with specific bilateral tax agreements with Denmark. Information about Denmark's double taxation agreements with other countries can be found on the Internet at: www.danzigerfdi.com/locations/denmark.

Housing

Students and visiting professors will find that house hunting in Denmark can be a daunting task. Rentals can be difficult to find throughout the year for the Danes. As you can imagine, the task becomes even more difficult for the foreigner searching at the start of an academic semester. Since availability is limited, it is a good idea to keep your expectations in check when looking for housing, especially in the larger cities such as Copenhagen, Århus and Odense.

Most homes in Denmark are personally owned, making rentals scarce. According to Danmarks Statistik (1997), 73% of all Danish housing is privately owned. Of that, only about one-third is available for rent. Approximately 20% of the housing is state or county owned. These apartments and houses are usually rented to people who have made it to the top of a very long waiting list. Although there are rentals out there, they are not that easy to find. Thus, it is incredibly difficult for foreigners to work through the official systems to find housing. Your best bet is to try to sublet an apartment or rent a room in someone's home.

Be prepared for differences in housing compared to what you are accustomed to in your own country. The bedrooms run small giving more space for the communal areas in Danish homes. In addition, kitchens and bathrooms are not as spacious as in other countries. In extreme cases, in some older apartment buildings all the residents may share the bathing facilities. However, Danish homes are no smaller than other European homes. In fact, the average two person living space is approximately 100 square meters.

In most cases, exchange students will find that the International Office of their host institution will assist in finding places for international students to live. You may be given the option of a room in a private home, a room in an apartment or house that you share with other students or a room in a Danish dormitory (*kollegium*). The International Office staff search diligently throughout the year for Danish families or landlords who are interested in renting or subletting to international students on a short-term basis. Since exchange students are usually in the country for less than six months, these leases are often difficult to find. The housing officer at your host institution will do his/her best to accommodate your wishes when it comes to housing.

Students pursuing Danish degrees, visiting faculty members and foreign employees will obviously want to rent apartments or homes for a longer period of time. Again, the International Office or personnel department of your institution is a good place to start to look for a place to live. It is also wise to contact the department where you will be studying/working to find out if they have any local information to help you in your search. Of course you can contact local real estate offices but it might be easier if you have someone from the university or college call on your behalf.

A third choice that has become more popular in recent years is relocation companies that assist in every detail, from start to finish, of a move abroad. Lastly, many rentals or sublets are posted on bulletin boards at grocery stores or the universities. In all cases, good quality rentals move quickly so do not hesitate to begin your apartment hunt early. See appendix 4 for addresses and services.

For those looking to join Danish society and really get to know a family, home-stay is a fantastic option. Home-stays usually include both room and board. You essentially become a member of the family. For those looking for a bit more privacy, renting a room in a private home allows you a glimpse into a regular family's life, without the obligations. In these cases, landlords rent out a room in their homes to supplement their own income. If you choose to live with a family, bear in mind that although you are paying rent, you are still a guest in the house. Whether you have a home-stay set up with both room and board or just rent a room in the house it is vital to establish a good relationship with your host family from the start. Never make assumptions about anything, no matter how trivial.

Many landlords and host families have strict rules for their tenants and do not allow, for example, students to entertain in their rooms, use the telephone for social calls or smoke in the house. Also, many of the university and college dormitories that are leased to students are located within residential areas. The neighbors of these buildings understand that students often keep unconventional hours and work and party into the wee hours of the morning. However, they are not very receptive to loud parties that disrupt the neighborhood. Obviously, the most successful relationships result from mutual respect. Thus, we recommend that both you and your landlord/host family reach an understanding of the ground rules early. This will save many headaches in the future.

Danish Addresses

Danish addresses are very logically written. Street names precede street numbers. After the street number comes the apartment floor number. The floor number may have a suffix which designates which side of the staircase the apartment sits: *tv* – on the left, *mf* – in the middle, *th* – on the right. The floors are numbered from the street level up. The ground floor is *stuen (st)* followed by 1st, 2nd, 3rd etc. Thus, an apartment address may read H. C. Andersens Boulevard 33, st. th. (33 H. C. Andersen's Boulevard, ground floor, on the right). Postal area codes (ZIP-codes) precede city names.

Daycare and Schools

Daycare

One issue that can greatly enhance your stay in a foreign country is the availability and security of good quality childcare. Denmark takes care of her children. As long as you get your name on a waiting list early enough, daycare in Denmark can be the working parent's dream. Danish municipalities (*kommuner*) are supposed to guarantee all parents (both employed and unemployed) daycare facilities for children of all ages. Naturally, as in any country, the political party in power and the resources available dictate the availability of these daycare services, however parents in Denmark can feel confident knowing that their children are safe in secure, well-established daycare centers run by trained personnel.

There are a wide variety of Danish daycare services. Below is a list with the typical options and prices of services available in most *kommuner*. The prices below are estimates based on the rates quoted from several different areas of the country. In addition, families with more than one child in daycare can have discounted rates (*søskenderabat* – 'sibling rebate'). Please note that availability of services and options as well as rates will vary from *kommune* to *kommune*. Table 3 shows typical rates for daycare services.

If you plan to take advantage of the state run daycare system, be aware that you cannot put your child's name on a waiting list before you establish residency in a *kommune*. The waiting time for a place in a daycare center can be as long as 3 – 6 months. There is a central unit (*pladsanvisning*) at each of the *kommune* offices that takes care of placing children in daycare centers. Reaction to foreigners varies from *kommune* to *kommune* so do not be surprised if assistance is not forthcoming on the part of the city workers. Like government workers worldwide, these people are doing the best they can in an overburdened system. However, with a little advanced action, you can alleviate the headaches. Thus, we suggest that you discuss your childcare needs with the administrative personnel at the institution where you will work and enlist their assistance in contacting the appropriate *kommune* offices.

Table 3. Daycare Service.

	Age	**Average Monthly Rate (kr.)**
Vuggestue (daycare center)	0-2 years	2000
Legestue (child/parent activity center)	6 months – 3 years	No charge
Børnehave (pre-school)	3-5/6 years	1300 (full time) 960 (part-time)
Dagpleje (in-home daycare)		1900
Børnehaveklasse (kindergarten)	6-7 years	No charge
Pasningsordning – skolefritidsordning (SFO) (on-site daycare at schools) SFO 1 SFO 2	6-10 10-12	1190 820
Fritidshjem (after school recreation center)	6-13	900
Fritidsklub (after school clubs)	12-16	155

Source: Frederiksberg Municipality. September 1998.

The language of the daycare centers is naturally Danish. There are a few English spoken daycare centers, but the demand for space is high. You can, however, assume that the majority of daycare service providers speak some English and will be able to communicate with you and your child through English. Due to the high level of foreign language proficiency in Denmark, you may be able to find a center for older children where other foreign languages are spoken, i.e. French, German, or Spanish but this should not be expected.

Schools

For many expatriates, enrolling your children into the regular school system is not an option. Since you may not intend to be in Denmark for more than a year or two you may want to send your child(ren) to one of the international schools where instruction takes place in English. The international schools provide a pre-kindergarten through International Baccalaureate program (grade 12). In most schools, Danish is taught to the children of all age groups and English as a second language instruction is available.

The school year in Denmark runs from mid August to mid June. In addition to their academic studies, students participate in a variety of cultural and recreational activities including trips both in Denmark and abroad. Public schools in Denmark for children are tuition free. However, the international schools in Denmark do charge tuition fees for their programs. Most of the international schools in Denmark are clustered around metropolitan Copenhagen.

The international schools run early education programs such as playgroup and kindergartens. The tuition fees for these programs range from 30,000 kr. to as high as 58,000 kr. a year (11 months). In some cases, parents can apply to their *kommune* for an assistance subsidy for these daycare programs. The subsidy can reduce the fees by almost 50%.

In regard to primary and secondary international school programs, tuition fees range from approximately 16,500 kr. to 50,000 kr. a school year. Prices for tuition for grades 10-12 tend to be higher – up to 80,000 kr. a year.

Making Social Connections

"... people here don't trust and talk to foreigners that much – it takes quite a lot of time to get 'under their skin.' But after that, they're really nice and even very talkative."
                    Martin Zubek, Czech Republic, student, age 22

Meeting new people and developing relationships can be difficult in any foreign country. The locals are busy at work and engaged with their old friends and their families. In Denmark, this is especially true. Danes tend to be a bit reserved when meeting new people or at least seldom take the initiative. But under the surface, the Danes can be very warm and generous. Many foreigners studying and working in Denmark have noted the difficulty they experienced in breaking into social circles and cliques. Much of this difficulty stems from the foreign approach to 'making friends and acquaintances' in Danish society. Unlike other nations where natural curiosity can bring people together and strike up conversation, e.g., an overheard foreign language or accent, a lost foreigner asking for directions, a single person at a cafe table, etc., in Denmark such opportunities for meeting is often passed by. Danes do not usually socialize with their colleagues from work or stop off for a drink with a co-worker on the way home. Nor do they automatically invite a new acquaintance home for a drink or a meal. There are various reasons for what seems cold, reserved behavior to the foreign observer.

To begin with, the family is very central to Danish life. Even though young people do move out on their own quite early compared to in other nations, they do not move far from their hometowns. In general, individuals tend not to move around much within Denmark. Students do regularly come to Copenhagen from other parts of the country or vice versa to pursue their education. In their new university town, these students tend to stick together with old friends from their hometown. After completing their studies, many of the students then move back to their hometowns. This helps to maintain strong relationships within the nuclear family and networks and lifelong friendships with others in the community. Thus, it can be difficult for a newcomer to enter into these well established social circles.

Danes tend to be a bit reserved. To meet them, join one of their clubs. They have for everything under the sun.

In addition to family, social clubs and organized activities are central to the Danish life. From early childhood Danes enlist schools and clubs for friendship and social development. A majority of activities stem from club outings or arrangements. People join clubs for everything under the sun – art clubs, theater clubs, language clubs, sports clubs, etc. Although individualism is alive and well in Denmark, societal affiliations are key to entertainment and friendship. Even in terms of dating, groups prevail. Young people tend to go to clubs and discos in groups, meet up with friends and break away in pairs as the night wears on only to meet up after the clubs close for breakfast at someone's home. Young and old alike will buy blocks of season tickets to the symphony or theater and attend concerts and performances with their old friends. These get-togethers can begin or are followed up at a cafe, restaurant or someone's home to promote the feeling of camaraderie and '*hygge*' (warmth/comfort/coziness).

With membership in club and social groups also comes a sense of individualism and independence. Although couples tend to live together much earlier than in many other nations, the independence of the individual is an essential element to Danish society. People will go to parties and socialize on their own without their partners. There is no stigma attached to showing up at a social event 'stag'. Therefore, do not assume that if you are invited to a party, that your partner is also invited. Always check with the person who invited you to a party before brining someone else along with you.

We can not rule out the weather as a factor when it comes to socializing. The climate does not invite chatting in the street or hanging out at street cafes. Sure enough, on a beautiful, sunny day the streets are packed with people talking and relaxing. But on those blustery, rainy days most Danes head indoors. Dark, cold winters bring people in for long dinners or afternoons occupied with cake and coffee. People usually invite friends from their clubs and social groups into their homes for warmth and '*hygge*'. The guest lists tend to be limited. Rarely will one meet a new face at one of these functions, as they tend to be for old friends and family.

Lastly, a side note to the Dane's reserved nature when it comes to receiving strangers is that the Danes are, in general, a well-traveled group. Unlike nations where the native population stays at home and waits for the world to come to them, Danes go out and see the world themselves. Opening any Sunday newspaper will attest to this. The plethora of charter tours and vacation packages to all parts of the world is overwhelming. With their high level of foreign language proficiency and formal education of world history, the Danes can travel abroad, speak to the natives in their own languages and get beyond the surface. Thus, we have a population of people who have, in a sense, sought out answers to questions of intercultural differences themselves. They have visited other countries personally and asked their questions on foreign soil. These world travelers have often fulfilled their need to know while abroad and have found the answers they were seeking. When they return to Denmark, they are not drawn to foreigners on their home soil for this is something to do while away. Although you would think that this enjoyment of foreign culture and language abroad would make people more curious about foreigners at home, once back in Denmark, the demands of everyday life and traditional Danish culture override. Despite the fact that various enclaves have melted into Danish society over the past several hundred years (Dutch merchants – 16th century, German civil servants – 17th century, Polish beet pickers – early 19th century and most recently Turkish guest workers – mid 20th century), until recently, few individual foreigners settled in Denmark so the culture lacks the tradition for receiving strangers into society.

As in all other countries that attract large numbers of visitors, foreigners in Denmark are inclined to gravitate to each other. This can be frustrating when you really want to interact with the natives. Given the Danes reserved nature and lack of contact with foreigners, how do *you* meet Danes in Denmark when you are coming from the outside? For exchange students and visiting academics, the natural place to start is at the university. The early days of the semester give students a chance to get to know each other and begin to form study groups. While faculty meetings and research groups give foreign professors chances to get to know each other. For those of you in companies and research centers, find out about clubs within the organization that others in your department participate in. Try to take advantage of these early opportunities to interact with the natives.

Language

The official language of Denmark is Danish. Danish is a northern Germanic language and is related to Icelandic, Faroese, Norwegian and Swedish. The language is rich in vowels. The variety of vowel sounds in Danish is typically the most difficult aspect of the language for the foreigner to wrap their vocal cords around. Most non-native speakers of Danish consider pronunciation difficult. The written language and the spoken language differ greatly. Danish is not a phonetic language. This makes it difficult to match sounds to their written form. The Danish alphabet is the Latin alphabet plus three extra letters added at the end: *Æ æ , Ø ø and Å å* .

As communicators, the Danes can be very direct. The language lacks many of the politeness expressions that other languages employ. For example, there is no Danish equivalent for the word 'please' although there are a number of phrases with this connotation. Thus, Danes, when communicating in for-

Danes frequently use sarcasm and irony to make their point, which is a part of the culture that must be decoded.

eign languages, have been considered impolite and rude by non-native speakers of Danish. In addition, Danes frequently use sarcasm and irony to make their point, which is another part of the culture that must be decoded. On the other hand, you will be hard pressed to find a culture where the people have more ways of saying 'thank you'.

"I was surprised at how little they said 'please,' until I realized that it's not impolite – they just don't have one word for 'please'. It is more in the intonation than the words."

Sarah West, England, student, age 19

English is the most common foreign language in the country. Children begin learning English in the fourth grade. Thus, by the time a student begins *gymnasium*, they will have had more than 8 years of formal training in the language. In addition, all English language films and television programs (except for the youngest children) are broadcasted in their original language with subtitles. Add the Internet to this factor and you get a society with constant exposure to the English language. This fact makes communication in English with the general population very easy.

Although it is convenient for the foreigner to communicate in English, it is worth the effort to learn as much Danish as possible. Understanding the language enables you to participate in Danish society at a deeper level. In general, Danes enjoy hearing foreigners struggle with the pronunciation of their language and are more than willing to help out and teach you a few words.

Body Language

The Danes have a bad reputation for being somewhat rude when it comes to 'common courtesy'. People do not generally say 'excuse me' or 'sorry' if they bump one another in a line or on the street. This should not be interpreted negatively and you should not take personal offence in such situations. The Danes just bump into each other and do not think much about it.

Smoking

In general, smoking is tolerated across the country at all levels of society. Although smokers have begun to ask for permission before lighting up, the general non-smoking public is still hesitant to deny this request. Actually, quite a large percentage of the population smokes. In 1998, Denmark ranked among the highest in terms of the percentage of female smokers compared to other European countries and the figures are rising.

Why do the Danes continue to smoke when the rest of the western world is trying to quit? Most smokers respond to this question by saying that they enjoy having a cigarette after a meal or at a party because it lends to the sense of *hygge* and is very relaxing. Smoking is considered a personal right and government interference in regard to restrictive legislation in this sphere is frowned upon. Each year, local authorities attempt to run campaigns to get people to quit smoking. In fact, there is even a designated 'Smoke Free Day' in Denmark.

In recent years, more and more focus has been placed on the issue of smoking in public places. Airports have begun to designate non-smoking areas and there is no smoking on domestic flights. Designated non-smoking areas in university offices and study areas also exist. However, smokers do not always respect non-smoking signs. It is not rare to see someone smoking while standing directly next to a 'No Smoking' sign.

If you are a non-smoker, be aware that outside of the university or workplace you may find yourself, more often than not, in the minority in Denmark.

Alcohol

Alcohol consumption is common in Danish society and beer is the national drink. Since Denmark is one of the biggest exporters of beer in the world, the Danes feel proud of their national drink. Beer is not reserved for special occasions and parties. There is little taboo associated with alcohol and many people consider beer, and more recently wine, appropriate for any occasion. At most university- or college cafeterias, you can buy beer all day long. There has however, been a noticeable change in the attitude towards having a beer for lunch in many places of work, especially where physical labor is being done. This, and an increasing tendency to drink wine among younger generations, has led to a considerable drop in beer consumption in Denmark.

Drinking beer and wine is another contributing factor in establishing *hygge* at a gathering or party. In the winter, people gather together to share a glass as a release from the long, cold, dark nights. In the summer, the drinks are served in celebration of the bright night skies and the opportunity to be outside. In general, the Danes like to have a good time and quickly find opportunities to toast a good occasion with '*skål*'.

For most, beer and Danish aquavit (*snaps*) are essential elements of a traditional Danish lunch. The traditional lunch spread consists of a collection of open-faced sandwiches (-*smørrebrød*) which can be artistic wonders. The sandwiches are put together from several fundamental elements – heavy dark rye bread (*rugbrød*) or French bread spread with a this layer of butter (*smørrebrød* literally means 'buttered bread') with fish, meat or cheese, usually eaten in that order. Marinated herring, fried plaice and homemade liver paté are popular favorites with *smørrebrød* connoisseurs. All of this, of course, is washed down with a cold Danish beer and perhaps a shot of *snaps*. They say that a shot of *snaps* is essential when eating herring because the fish needs something to swim in!

Although drinking alcohol is normally socially acceptable, there are stiff regulations when it comes to drinking and driving. Penalties for driving under the influence deter people from drinking and driving. Most people choose to leave their cars at home or designate a driver before going to a party or traditional lunch (which can last from 4-6 hours!).

Dinner Parties and Other Celebrations

If you are fortunate enough to get invited to a meal or party be prepared to stay for more than just a couple of hours. Many

Dinner Parties and Other Celebrations 69

visitors to Denmark have found themselves in the awkward position of leaving dinner parties too early, due to commitments they have made thinking that a dinner called for 7:00 pm would be over by 10:00 pm. You can expect that the average sit-down dinner will run for at least four hours, with more formal events such as birthday parties or anniversary celebrations lasting as long as 8-10 hours. This is also true for an informal lunch invitation. If you are invited to lunch at 12:00 or 1:00, do not make dinner plans for that evening. Most likely you will not be leaving your host before at least 4:00 or 5:00 that evening and you will not be hungry!

The social customs at private dinner parties in Denmark may be more formal than you are accustomed to in your own culture. It is not rare to have designated seating (with name cards), china and candles on the table for what you thought was a casual, friendly average Friday night dinner. Although the dress code remains casual at a Danish dinner, the social code is understood. To begin with, a Dane will rarely show up empty-handed to someone's home if invited for a meal. The most common gifts for the host are flowers, a bottle of wine or some small token. Secondly, punctuality is a mainstay of Danish culture. If dinner is called for 7:00 pm, you are expected to arrive at 7:00 pm or a few minutes after. Dinner will usually start within 10-15 minutes of the last guest's arrival. Lastly, you will note that guests will repeatedly thank the host, complement the food and show polite appreciation throughout the evening for the host's efforts. In fact, one of the most important phrases will learn shortly your arrival in Denmark will be *'tak for mad'* (thank you for the meal) which is at the end of a meal to thank the host. All the same rules apply for pot-luck dinners, but they will usually be more informal in terms of seating.

At a dinner you will most likely be treated to a variety of homemade specialties. The host will prepare for hours to present you with a home-cooked meal. In the most extreme cases, the host will spend days preparing the meal and often go as far as baking the bread or making homemade ice cream.

Danes love their food and will talk about a great meal for weeks to come.

In regard to the food, the foreign guest should be prepared to not only sit for a long time but also eat for a long time. Traditionally, you will be served a light first course (usually fish) followed by the main course (usually some type of meat) and ending with dessert (often an ice cream dish). Coffee will not be served until well after dessert has been cleared away and then you will be served cake and cookies along side. Following cake and coffee comes the chips and drinks. At big celebrations, just in case you have not had your share by the end of the party, the host will serve up open face sandwiches (*smørrebrød*) or hot soup to send you on your way. This midnight snack, which usually takes place around 2:00 or 3:00 in the morning, is rightfully called 'night food' (*natmad*). A word to the wise – pace yourself. The courses will make several appearances around the table. Take small portions to start since you will probably be offered second and sometimes even third helpings of these wonderful dishes.

As mentioned above, the Danes put great emphasis on celebrating good times and special occasions. Parties for birthdays of years ending in zero (e.g. 30, 40, 50 …), weddings, and special anniversaries bring large groups of people together for big parties with strings of speeches and songs (written to a popular tune especially for the guest(s) of honor). Although some friends and family members may take the opportunity to make impromptu speeches, most of these toasts are prepared speeches which can last quite a while. Although the speeches and songs are primarily written in Danish, it can be fun for the foreign guest to sit back and observe the entire event. You might find it hard to believe that this is the same nationality described above as 'cool' and 'reserved'. The Danes will conclude each song and speech with several hearty cheers of 'hurrah, hurrah, hurrah' and '*skål*'. Following the official '*skål*' come all the traditional '*skål*' songs. Everyone knows these and will join in with great enthusiasm.

No occasion will pass without a reception to bring co-workers together, an ideal opportunity to meet the Danes in a relaxed atmosphere.

Hygge in the Workplace

Lunch

The mid-day is a time for everyone to stop what they are doing and meet together for a quick lunch. Besides being an opportunity to take a break, lunch is taken very seriously across the country. Most universities and colleges have cafeterias which serve both hot and cold food, *smørrebrød* and drinks. Although subsidized a bit by the institution, the prices can run on the expensive side for cafeteria food (although cheap compared to restaurant prices). Therefore, many students and staff members will bring along a bag lunch from home.

Special Occasions

Guest professors and Ph.D. students will find that their colleagues will also try to bring *hygge* into the workplace. No occasion will pass without a reception to bring co-workers together. The anniversary of a department, the retirement of a co-worker or the 50th birthday of a professor are all examples of occasions which draw everyone out of their offices into a central location for the traditional speeches and toasts. These small parties offer an opportunity for administrators and academic staff members to meet together in an unofficial capacity and get to know one another. It is a good idea to try to attend as many of these functions as you can, as this is an ideal opportunity to meet the Danes in a relaxed atmosphere.

"I can vividly remember when I stumbled upon an office wine reception. I was walking past a common work area between two departments on a Friday afternoon and I noticed a circle of people gathered around a candle-lit table giving speaches with glasses raised. The group was celebrating a newly founded cooperation between two departments. At first this function seemed very formal and stiff but now that I have been here for a while I have come to look forward to these ritual gatherings."

American visiting professor, age 34

Voices of Experience

By Julianna Hsuan*

I am one of those few who claim no particular place in this world as home. Having lived in many countries including Brazil, Taiwan, U. S. A. and Finland, I must say that residing in Denmark is truly an experience of its own! So what is my perception of Denmark after having been here for a couple of months?

If one likes pastry and bread, Denmark is heaven! There is no place on earth that can match Denmark when it comes to freshly baked goods, especially in the morning. The selection is unbelievable... from white to full-grain breads, not to mention the ones made with vegetables and nuts. Simply put, Danes are creative bakers!

For those who like nature and culture, Denmark is a paradise. There are parks, museums and castles everywhere. But beware of dog 'poo-poos' if one takes a walk to these places. It can be very annoying coming home with your shoes full of this stuff...

Unlike the U.S. and some other countries to some degree, one does not need to have a car in order to get around Denmark. The transportation infrastructure is terrific! Trains and busses run around the clock and are fairly punctual. Driving in Denmark, however, requires a change of attitude. One always has to pay extra attention not to run over the bikers. Did I mention that the traffic coming from the right hand side always has right of way, unless otherwise specified?

* Julianna Hsuan is a visiting researcher. Originally from Taiwan, Julianna was raised in Brazil and educated in the United States. She resides in Finland with her husband and is spending an academic year in Denmark.

Driving in Denmark, one has to pay extra attention not to run over the bikers.

There are also a few not-so-pleasant and difficult-to-get-used-to adjustments in Denmark. For instance, one can hardly find a 'non-smoking' area in public places. It also seems that the majority of smokers are women. Why? I don't know. Maybe because the Queen also enjoys smoking?

Living in Denmark can be quite expensive, though. Eating out is often saved for special occasions. The price of food is comparable with Finland, but extremely high relative to other non-Scandinavian countries. Shopping for food can be nerve racking sometimes. There are virtually millions of specialty shops in Copenhagen and its suburbs. It also seems that every grocery store carries its own unique goods. It is not unusual to shop at a few stores before one can find and be satisfied with the goods needed in order to prepare a decent meal. The concept of hypermarket appears to be almost non-existent.

From a Finnish perspective, can I assume that Danes and

Finns share similar culture? Well, to some extent the answer is yes. Take alcoholic beverages, for instance. Danes, like their Scandinavian counterparts, are not exactly proud of their drinking habits. They have a tremendous ability to consume all kinds of booze and stay sober (at least that is how it appears to be) at social gatherings. Of course, the ability to drink matches their ever-lasting stamina for partying. That's not all... Beer and wine are also sold at company and university cantinas! Needless to say, drinking during any meal is a socially acceptable behavior. The same can not be said about American or Asian cultures.

Coming from a Latin background, Danes may seem rude and cold at times. I think it is derived from the impression that they always carry a serious expression on their faces. I always have to remind myself not to hug (definitely not kiss as we do in Latin countries) a Dane the first time I meet him or her. On the other hand, having lived in Finland for five years, Danes are quite friendly (the shyness of Finns is often mistaken as rudeness). Just about everyone can speak English, making the transition and adaptation of living in Denmark much easier!

Oh! I must add a comment on Danish language. In most languages, words can be pronounced the way they are written. The Danish language, on the other hand, does not get the prize for the most logical language (at least in its pronunciation) in the world. The written language seems so alien from the spoken language! Needless to say, learning Danish can be a real challenge. Besides, one can get around without knowing any Danish, as they all can communicate extremely well in English.

I am sure my perception will change as I spend this year as a visiting scholar at the Copenhagen Business School. Who knows?! I may even be able to speak Danish. There is no doubt in my mind that this is going to be a magnificent year!

*By David Fink**

I started my adventure in Denmark by taking the bus from the airport to the bleak Copenhagen University at Amager campus with the other exchange students where we would all be matched with our new families for the next several months. As we were taken away one by one by our newly adopted parents we had no idea where we were going or what new experiences would have. I quickly found that my the family treated me like one of their own. I had the freedom to come and go as I wanted and felt included in all the traditions that the family had made part of their daily lives. By living with the families most of the secrets of Danish life were exposed. This was my primary link to Danish culture.

After initially settling in we all went off to explore Copenhagen. In the beginning trying to feel our way around in a new city we would all go out in large groups to cafes, museums and shops. Quickly we learned that this was no way to assimilate into a new society. Danes would run out of our way to avoid our stampeding groups. We also found that it would be just like being at home at the universities we had left behind. Going out with old friends from school was not the experience we were after. Soon we started to go places in groups of no larger than two or three. We found it still it was difficult to meet Danes but at least this would give us a better chance. The only way we could meet people was by approaching them. We felt a bit forward but it was well worth the extra effort. Typically after

---

* David Fink was an exchange student to Denmark in 1990 with the DiS Program at the University of Copenhagen. David is now an architect and has recently returned to Denmark to work in his field.

breaking the ice there would only be a brief conversation. On a few occasions we would have long conversations with people that we meet. Mostly this would be our only meeting. Sometimes we would meet again. To have them take us around Copenhagen was an experience that could never be found in the best guide books. The Danes that we met regularly would help you in any way at any time.

After I had a small group that I knew, I started to be invited to parties. In Denmark people can find almost anything to celebrate. Sometimes they start with a meal that can last several hours. Parties will go late into the night and involve lots of beer and food. These were the best places to meet people. This is where you will also find that the Danes have a great sense of humor. At parties people sing songs that have been written just for that occasion and often speeches are made. If you know Danish at these times you will be well rewarded.

One of the most difficult tasks was learning Danish. With its very precise pronunciation and that almost everyone speaks English fluently makes learning the language even more difficult. Since my stay in Copenhagen was just for a short period of time, leaning Danish was not a priority and very few people in my group took classes. In the beginning I started taking Danish classes, but after attempting to use Danish and having responses back primarily in English it did not seem worth the effort. Afterward, I regretted this decision to stop taking Danish classes. Like any society there is a lot of the culture that is based on the language and to be able to have access to it makes life easier and more enjoyable.

Life in Copenhagen was very good even despite the long hours of darkness and the dismal weather at the beginning of our stay. Since I arrived in January the days quickly grew longer. You could see the change almost daily. As the days grew longer, the happier the people became and the city came alive to fully take advantage of this change. The Danes came out to worship the return of the sun.

I found the standard of life to be high. The adjustment to the new lifestyle was not difficult. When it was time to go home everyone in the group was sad to leave. We brought some of the new way of life home with us. We all said we would return as I have done several times since my first stay.

By Anne Fabricius*

I came to live in Denmark at the age of twenty-five. My personal circumstances meant that I expected that the move to Denmark would be permanent. I was married to a Dane, had a small child, and was moving partly for professional reasons, partly for family reasons.

I had grown up in subtropical Australia, in southern Queensland, an area which differed from Denmark in a multitude of ways. The year-round outdoor lifestyle which was the mainstay of my childhood was not the only contrast. I came from a society which only in the 1970s began to shrug off the 'cultural cringe', its feeling of Australian inferiority stemming from convict origins of only two hundred years ago. I came to Denmark, whose people live surrounded by marks of long human habitation in Scandinavia. I still have vivid memories of the experience of touching the walls of a medieval church for the first time!

The first three years of living in Denmark were spent on an acclimatization process that I can not imagine myself going through again! I had to learn a new language, a new culture, and it wasn't just me: I had a dependent child as well. I remember wondering how I would cope with a doctor's visit with a sick child and my faltering Danish. At the time I came to live here permanently, I could put simple sentences together in Danish, but there were large gaps in my knowledge. From one day to the next, I decided that I would attempt to speak Danish to Danes, no matter how many mistakes I made. In a way it

---

* Anne Fabricius is currently a Ph.D. student at the Copenhagen Business School. Anne is from Australia and lives in Denmark with her husband and two small children.

was made easier by the fact that I was living in a small country community on Funen, where people were not willing to speak much English to me.

I had experienced Danish summer before I came to live here, but not the Danish winter, especially not the period from January to April. That first year, I would hear people say "Well, spring is on the way" and thinking "but this weather feels like winter to me..." not realizing that people were looking out for other things: the first crocuses, migrating birds... Perhaps the reality of the climate should have dawned on me when I wondered why my husband's childhood photos were so often taken indoors. I think I have now started to see the weather with Danish eyes, and I grab the opportunity of a day outdoors when it comes.

After several years mostly caring for small children, I began as a part-time teacher at Copenhagen Business School. I taught first-year classes in written and oral English, the latter with a large element of phonetics, which I had studied as a linguistics student in Australia. Phonetics gradually interested me more and more, and after half a year I applied to do a Ph.D. in sociolinguistic phonetics.

One significant difference between Denmark and Australia has a great deal of bearing on my life at present. The fact that childcare for preschool children is well organized and supervised by local councils means that I can feel secure in delivering my children to the care of professional people full-time, to enable me to work the hours I do. Although the situation is improving all the time, childcare for preschoolers in Australia is largely private and expensive, and difficult to obtain full-time. Thus, the workforce participation rate for women with pre-school children is much lower in Australia than it is in Denmark.

Life as a Ph.D. student at CBS differs somewhat from my experience as an M.A. student in Australia. Perhaps this is partly due to my own home life and responsibilities, and it's not uncommon for Ph.D. students here to have houses and families! I think it's also due to the rather different nature of universities in Denmark. As an M.A. student I lived in a residential college on campus, close to lecture halls, academic departments and many facilities for shopping, sports and social life. The CBS campus is spread over a wide area in Frederiksberg, and you can't buy a tube of toothpaste in the one shop in Dalgas Have. I think this makes for a sharper distinction between 'work' and 'home' life for students here in Denmark than there was in Australia when I was a student there.

*By Roy Langer**

I just returned to Denmark from a extended research visit at a German university. I cannot tell you, how happy I am to be back. I really appreciate the advantages of Danish universities in comparison to those in Germany, where the conditions for study are comparatively bad: libraries are poorly equipped (partly due to a lack of money, partly because of books get stolen); computer facilities are almost absent; the personal contact between the many students and the few university professors is almost non-existent and the general pedagogical orientation seems to be the same as the one that died out in Denmark many years ago. Students in Germany had to wait for the chance to attend obligatory courses for one or even two years, because these courses were overbooked. Classes were overcrowded and schedules were literally not student-friendly.

I remember having had the same feeling of liberation and revelation when I started studying in Denmark about a decade ago. The equipment, the organization and administration of study and the pedagogical thinking were considerably different from what I had experienced during my studies in Germany. Danish students have a remarkable influence on form, content and evaluation of their studies. The social relationship between professors and students had a profoundly different character: instead of top-down-communication and hierarchy, in Denmark I experienced my professors as guides and tutors, who treated me as an equal and understood their own role as the

* *Roy Langer is an assistant professor at the Copenhagen Business School in the Institute for Intercultural Communication and Management. Roy is German and has lived in Denmark for a number of years.*

one of an older (and more knowing) supervisor of my professional development. Project and teamwork as one of the fundamental organizing principles replaced the lectures and seminars I was used to in Germany. The whole atmosphere in Denmark appeared to me much more informal and relaxed.

Today, almost ten years later, my view on studying and working on Danish universities is more shaded and ambiguous – due to my personal experiences from studies, teaching and research in different institutions. First of all, differences between the institutions have to be pointed out: students and academic work differs a lot, depending on what subjects you study and which university you attend. There are considerable institutional differences between e.g. the old universities in Copenhagen and Århus, business schools and a reform university like Roskilde University Center – both with regard to the form and the content and the whole academic culture around the studies. It is very difficult to make generalizations. But whereas the old universities might be described as those institutions, respecting the classical academic virtues in terms of form and content of teaching and research most, business schools are very focussed on empirical applications of academic life to commercial and social issues and a reform university like Roskilde University Center focuses on those organizational principles for university teaching (e.g. project organization) that are a result of the educational reforms of the 1970s.

Although the educational policy in Denmark has made great efforts to broaden the social background of Danish students in higher education, a recent study showed that most of the students have an academic family background. There also are certain elitist tendencies at Danish universities, depending on the subject of study, because the pre-requirements and pre-capabilities to get a study place are different for the different subjects.

Despite of my positive comments in the beginning, my own studies and work at Danish universities also illuminated some of the – from my own perspective – rather problematic aspects of academic life in Denmark. The social orientation of studies, coming into presence by a great deal of project work, also has disadvantages – especially for students with a weak image or newcomers from abroad: the establishment of student project groups can sometimes be compared with an end-of-season dance, where certain students are frozen out.

Even the basically positive aspects of democracy, informality and students influence on their study can have shady sides or disadvantages. For instance, being critical (a basic approach which Danish students already learn in primary education) is getting to be the only content of academic work; the relationship between professors and students is almost of therapeutic character, instead of an analytical knowledge-relationship; and formal aspects of the study (e.g. whether the schedule of lectures and seminars suites to students personal schedule including other interests such as part-time jobs, hobbies etc., whether the teachers put holes in handouts or whether teachers are entertaining in the classroom) are moving focus from content aspects of academic work.

Despite of these critical comments, studying and working in Danish higher education would be an interesting, enlightening and experience for everyone. It is easy to establish (also personal) relationships to Danes through academic work. Language – especially if you can communicate in English – is normally not a problem. The quality of teaching and research is normally high – although in some subjects almost exclusively inspired and orientated towards the English speaking world and neglecting scientific achievements and debates in Germany, France or other parts of the world. Last but not least there are lots of social activities around university life in Denmark: sport clubs, parties, student clubs, political organizations – or just the ritual and almost obligatory "Friday beer" in the students club at the end of an academic week.

Appendix 1:
Traditional and Legal Holidays

The Danes do not necessarily need legal or religious holidays to have an occasion to celebrate, but it is always a good excuse. Try to get involved in the festivities of the local holidays and find out about the traditions and customs for yourself. Below we have listed most of the Danish holidays and a little information about what you might expect from the day. (Those holidays marked with an asterisk * are considered public holidays.)

New Year's Day – January 1* (Nytårsdag): All the shops and businesses are closed in celebration of the new year (and to recover from the night before) and people tend to stay close to home. In the evening, the Prime Minister addresses the nation via a live television broadcast.

Shrovetide (Fastelavn's dag): This is the Sunday before Lent and the occasion is celebrated with costumes and the eating of special rolls (fastelavns-boller) across the country. The holiday has its origin in the belief that evil can be driven away by killing a cat. With this in mind, children dress up in costumes and participate in the ritual of 'knocking a cat out of a barrel' (slå katten af tønden). Today, the cat is made of cardboard and sits atop a wooden barrel. The event is similar to children attacking a Mexican piñata.

Easter
Although not a strongly religious country, Denmark takes the Easter holidays quite seriously. The country essentially closes

down for approximately 5 days as the Danes honor this period. Many families decorate their homes with Easter eggs, chicks and bunnies.

The Easter holiday comprises:
- *Palm Sunday** (Palmesøndag): The Sunday before Easter, celebrated in commemoration of Christ's triumphal entry into Jerusalem.
- *Maundy Thursday** (Skærtorsday): The Thursday before Easter, celebrated in commemoration of Christ's Last Supper and His washing of the disciples feet on that day.
- *Good Friday** (Langfredag): The Friday before Easter, observed as the anniversary of the Crucifixion of Christ.
- *Easter Sunday** (Påskedag): The day celebrated in commemoration of the resurrection of Christ.
- *Easter Monday** (2. Påskedag): also a public holiday.

Great Prayer Day (Store bededag): The 4th Friday after Easter, established by Christian VI to reduce the number of official days of prayer (days away from work) throughout the year. Thus, he proclaimed one long day of prayer.

May 1* (arbejdernes internationale kampdag): The socialist parties hold demonstrations and political rallies throughout the country. Most workplaces close at 12:00 noon.

Ascension Day (Kristi himmelfartsdag): The 40th day after Easter, celebrated in commemoration of the ascension of Christ.

Pentecost or Whitsun (Pinsedag;): The 7th Sunday after Easter, celebrated in commemoration of the descent of the Holy Spirit on the day of Pentecost.

Whitmonday* (2. Pinsedag): A public holiday.

Constitution Day*: (Grundlovsdag): On June 5, 1849, Denmark established its first constitution. This day marked the beginning of the Danish democracy. This day is traditionally a day for political rallies, parades and picnics.

Mid-Summer's Eve (Sankt Hans aften): The evening of June 23 is celebrated around a bonfire. Friends and neighbors gather to light the fire and burn a witch (usually built from kindling) that has been placed atop. Everyone cheers as the witch (the cause of all evil) burns and traditional songs are sung. This is not a public holiday.

Morten Bisp: This day is celebrated on November 11 in commemoration of Martin Luther. The night before (Mortensaften), Danes traditionally dine on goose or duck and give thanks. This is not a public holiday.

Christmas Eve* (Juleaften): On December 24, many families celebrate Christamas Eve at home. Traditionally, the Danes eat goose, duck or roast pork (flæskesteg) with a variety of trimmings and rice pudding (ris á la mande) for dessert. After dinner, people dance around the Christmas tree and sing songs. Each family usually has songbooks for this occasion.

Christmas Day & *December 26* *(1. juledag & 2. juledag): December 25 tends to be a day to be with family and friends. Businesses and shops are closed and the Danes spend the day visiting each other to share a glass of wine or beer and spread holiday wishes. December 26 is also public holiday.

The general population actively participates in the festivities of the Christmas season in Denmark. From the start of December, the feeling of the holidays is in the air. Most companies and businesses have traditional Christmas lunches (*julefrokost*) where the employees gather to share in the holiday cheer. These lunches tend to be almost identical from office to office, with traditional foods, speeches and songs written especially for the occasion and a lot of beer and snaps.

December 31: New Year's Eve (Nytårs-aften) is celebrated with vigor in Denmark. The evening traditionally starts at 6:00 pm when the entire country essentially comes to a standstill to watch the televised speech of Queen Margrethe and drink the first toast of the evening. Although the traditional food of the evening is poached cod (*kogt torsk*) most people take the opportunity to splurge on New Year's Eve and have lavish dinner parties with a great deal of wine and champagne. Midnight usually brings people back to the television where they will see and hear the clock at Copenhagen's City Hall chime and listen to a choir sing the hymn 'Welcome, Year of Our Lord' (*Vær velkommen, Herrens år*). Luckily, the text for this is written on the TV screen so that you can join and all of the not-so-holy Danes can join in! From the moment the clock strikes midnight, Denmark is alight with fireworks. Individuals drinking champagne spill into the streets to ignite and admire the fireworks going on all around them.

Appendix 2:
Royal Danish Embassies and Consulates

Argentina
Real Embajada de Dinamarca
Avenida Leandro N. Alem 1074, 1001 Buenos Aires
Tel: + (1) 312 6901.   Fax: 00-54 (1) 312 7857
Telex: 22173

Australia
Royal Danish Embassy
Canberra 15 Hunter Street
Yarralumla, A.C.T. 260, Canberra
Tel: + (6) 273 2195/96.   Fax: + (6) 273 3864

Royal Danish Consulate General
Gold Fields House
1 Alfred St., Circular Quay, SYDNEY NSW 2000
Tel: (02) 92447 2224.   Fax: (02) 9251 7504
e-mail: dkconsul@dkconsul-sydney.org.au

Austria
Königlich Dänische Botschaft
Führichgasse 6, 1015 Wien
Mail address: Postfach 298, 1015 Wien
Tel: + 43 (1) 512 7904.   Fax: + 43 (1) 513 8120

Bangladesh
Royal Danish Embassy of Dhaka
Royal Danish Embassy
House #1, Road #51, Gulshan-2, Dhaka-1212
Tel: + 880-2-881799.   Fax: + 880-2-883638
e-mail: dandhaka@citechco.net

Belgium
Ambassade Royale de Danemark
1 Avenue Louise 221, Bte. 7, B-1050 Bruxelles
Tel: + 32 (2) 626 0770.   Fax: + 32 (2) 647 0709
Telex: 22591

Brazil
Royal Danish Embassy
Embaixada Real de Dinmarca
SES – Avenida das Nacões, lote 26, 70416 -900 Brasília D.F.
Mail address: Caixa Postal 0484
70359-970 Brasília D.F.
Tel: + 55 (61) 242 8188.   Fax: + 55 (61) 244 5245

Royal Danish Consulate General in São Paulo
Rua Oscar Freire, 379 – cj.31, 01426-001 São Paulo – SP
Tel: + 55 11 3061 3625.   Fax: + 55 11 3068 9867
e-mail: dkconsul@denmark.org.br

Bulgaria
Royal Danish Embassy
SofiaBoulevard Tsar Osvoboditel 10, 4th floor
Mail address: P.O. Box 1393, Sofia 1000
Tel: + 00-359 (2) 980 0830.   Fax: + 00-359 (2) 980 0831

Canada
Royal Danish Embassy
Ottawa 47 Clarence Street, Suite 450, Ottawa
Ontario K1N 9K1
Tel: + 1 (613) 562 1812.   Fax: + 1 (613) 562 1811

Appendix 2: Royal Danish Embassies and Consulates 91

Danish General Consulate
151 Bloor Street West, Suite 310
Toronto, Ontario, Canada, M5S 1S4
Tel: (416) 962-5661.   Fax: (416) 962-3668
e-mail: hyperlink mailto:danish@tradecomm.com

The Czech Republic
Royal Danish Embassy
Maltézské námesti 5, 118 01 Praha 1, Malá Strana
Mail address.: P.O. Box 25, 118 01 Praha 1, Malá Strana
Tel: + 420 (2) 5731 6630, (2) 5731 6640, (2) 5731 6639
Fax: + 420 (2) 2431 1946

China
Royal Danish Embassy in Beijing
1 Dong Wu Jie, San Li Tun, 100600 Beijing
People's Republic of China.
Tel: + 86 (10) 6532 2431.   Fax: + 86 (10) 6532 2439
E-mail: ambadan@public.bta.net.cn
www.dk-embassy-cn.org/

Danish General Consulate
Room 701, Shanghai International Trade Centre,
No. 2200 Yan'an Xi Lu, Shanghai 200335
Tel: 021- 6209 0500.   Fax: 021- 6209 0504
e-mail: gkldksh@uninet.com.cn

England
Royal Danish Embassy of London
55 Sloane Street, London SW1X 9SR
Tel: 0171 333 0212/0210.   Fax: 0171 333 0275

Estonia
Royal Danish Embassy of Tallinn
Rävala Pst. 9, 6th floor, EE-15047 Tallinn
Tel: + 372 6313 120.   Fax: + 372 6313 351
Telex: 173262 AMDAN .
e-mail: hyperlink mailto:dan.emb@online.ee

Finland
Royal Danish Embassy
Helsingfors Centralgatan 1, FIN- 00100 Helsingfors
Mail address. P.M. 1042, FIN- 00101 Helsingfors
Tel: + 358 (0) 17 17 41.   Fax: + 358 (0) 17 15 11

France
Royal Danish Embassy
Ambassade Royale du Danemark
77 Avenue Marceau, F – 75 116 Paris
Tel: + 33 (1) 44 31 21 87.   Fax: + 33 (1) 44 31 21 21

Royal Danish General Consulate
Kgl. Dansk Generalkonsulat
2, rue Henri Barbusse, B.P. 2136
13205 Marseille Cedex 1, France
Tel.: + 33 4 91 90 80 23.   Fax: + 33 4 91 91 35 00

Germany
Royal Danish Embassy in Bonn
Kgl. Dänische Botschaft Bonn
Pfälzer Straße 14, D-53111 Bonn
Postfach 18 02 20, D-53032 Bonn
Tel: (0228) 72 99 10.   Fax: (0228) 72 99 131
e-mail: botschaft@daenemark.org

Royal Danish Embassy of Berlin
Kgl. Dänische Botschaft Außenstelle Berlin
Wichmannstr. 5, D-10787 Berlin
Postfach 30 12 45, D-10722 Berlin
Tel: (030) 25 00 10.   Fax: (030) 25 00 11 90
e-mail: hyperlink mailto:berlin@daenemark.org

Danish General Consulate
Dänisches Generalkonsulat
Sendlinger-Tor-Platz 10, D-80336 München
Tel.: + 49 (0) 89 54 58 54 12.   Fax: + 49 (0) 89 59 78 15
e-mail: dk-munchen@t-online.de

Greece
Royal Danish Embassy
Athen 11 Vas. Sofias, GR- 106 71 Athens
Tel: + 30 (1) 363 6163.   Fax: + 30 (1) 360 8315

Hungary
Ambassade Royale de Danemark
Budapest XII, Határör út 37, 1122 Hungary
Tel: + 36 (1) 1557 320.   Fax: + 36 (1) 1753 803

Hong Kong
Hong Kong Special Administrative Region
Suite 2402 B, Great Eagle Centre,
23 Habour Road, Wanchai, Hong Kong
Tel: + 852 2827 8101.   Fax: + 852 2827 4555
e-mail: danconhk@netvigator.com

India
Royal Danish Embassy
New Delhi 11, Aurangzeb Road, New Delhi 110 011
Tel: + 91 (11) 301 0961.   Fax: + 91 (11) 301 0900

Iran
Royal Danish Embassy
P.O. Box 19395-5358, Tehran, Islamic Republic of Iran
Tel: + 98 (21) 26 13 63 / + 98 (21) 26 70 20
Fax: + 98 (21) 203 00 07
e-mail: ambadane.teheran@inet.uni2.dk

Ireland
Royal Danish Embassy
121-122 St. Stephen's Green, Dublin 2
Tel: + 353 (1) 475 6404.   Fax: + 353(1) 478 4536

Israel
Royal Danish Embassy of Tel Aviv
23, Bnei Moshe Street, P.O. Box 21 080, Tel Aviv 61 210
Tel: + 972 (0)3 544 2144/45.   Fax: + 972 (0)3 546 5502
e-mail: hyperlink mailto:dkemb@netvision.net.il

Italy
Ambasciata di Danimarca
Via dei Monti Parioli 50, I – 00197 Roma
Tel: + 39 (6) 3610 290.   Fax: + 39 (6) 3200 441

Japan
Royal Danish Embassy of Tokyo
29-6 Sarugaku-cho, Shibuya-ku, Tokyo 150 0033
Tel: + 81 3 3496 3001.   Fax: + 81 3 3496 3440
e-mail: dkembtokyo@twics.com

Latvia
Royal Danish Embassy
Liela Pils iela 11, LV-1863 Riga
e-mail: amdkriga@amdkriga.org.lv
Tel: + 37 17 226 210 / 37 17 210 433
Fax: + 37 17 820 234 / 37 17 229 218

Lithuania
Royal Danish Embassy
Vilnius T. Kosciuskos gatvé 36, Vilnius
Tel: + 37090 30 110

Luxembourg
Ambassade Royale du Danemark
Luxembourg 4, Boulevard Royal, L – 2449 Luxembourg
Tel: + 35 222 21 24.   Fax: + 35 222 21 22

Appendix 2: Royal Danish Embassies and Consulates 95

Malaysia
Royal Danish Embassy of Kuala Lumpur
Wisma Denmark
22nd Floor, 86 Jalan Ampang, 50450 Kuala Lumpur,
P.O. Box 10908, 50728 Kuala Lumpur
Tel: + 60 3 202 2001.   Fax. + 60 3 202 2012/2015
e-mail: denmark@rdembsy.po.my

The Netherlands
Royal Danish Embassy
Koninginnegracht 30, 2514 AB Den Haag
Mail address: Postbus 85654, 2508 CJ Den Haag
Tel: + 31 (70) 302 5959.   Fax: + 31 (70) 360 2150

New Zealand
See Australia

Norway
Den kgl. Danske ambassade i Oslo
Olav Kyrres gate 7, N-0244 Oslo
Tel: + 47 22 54 08 00.   Fax: + 47 22 55 46 34
e-mail: danske@online.no

Poland
Royal Danish Embassy
Warszawa Ul. Rakowiecka 19, PL – 02-517 Warszawa
Tel: + 48 (22) 48 75 80.   Fax: + 48 (22) 48 26 00

Portugal
Embaixada Real da Dinamarca
Rua Castilho 14-3o, 296 Lisboa Codex
Tel: + 351 (1) 35 45 099, (1) 35 45 124, (1) 35 45 249, (1) 35 45
607, (1) 35 45 966.   Fax: + 351(1) 35 70 124

Russia
Royal Danish Embassy
9 Prechistensky Pereulok, 119034 Moscow
Tel: + 7 (095) 201 7860, (095) 201 7868, (095) 201 2227, (095) 201 2232.   Fax: + 7 (095) 201 5357
E-mail: dkembmos@glasnet.ru

Singapore
Royal Danish Embassy of Singapore
101 Thomson Rd
#13-01/02 United Square, Singapore 307591
Tel: (65) 250 3383.   Fax: (65) 253 3764

The Slovak Republic
See The Czech Republic

Spain
Embajada Real de Dinamarca
Claudio Coello 91, 28006 Madrid
Tel: + 34(1) 431 8445.   Fax: + 34(1) 431 9168

Sweden
Kgl. Dansk Ambassade
Jakobs Torg 1, Box 1638, 111 86 Stockholm
Tel: + 46 (8) 406 75 00.   Fax: + 46(8) 791 72 20

Switzerland
Ambassade Royale de Danemark
Thunstrasse 95, 3006 Bern
Tel: + 41 (31) 352 5011.   Fax: + 41 (31) 351 2395
e-mail :botschaft@denmark.ch
embassy@denmark.ch
www.denmark.ch

The United States of America
Royal Danish Embassy Washington
3200 Whitehaven Street, N.W. Washington, D.C. 20008-3683
Tel: + 1 (202) 234 4300.   Fax: + 1 (202) 328 1470
e-mail :ambadane@erols.com
www.denmarkemb.org

Venezuela
Royal Danish Embassy Caracas
Embajada de Dinamarca
Torre Centuria, piso 7
Avenida Venezuela/Calle Mohedano, El Rosal, Caracas
Tel.: (+ 58 2) 951 46 18/ 56 06 / 66 18.   Fax: (+ 58 2) 951 52 78
e-mail: danmark@internet.ve

Appendix 3: Institutions of Higher Education

All universities are listed but, for space reasons, selected colleges are listed for each field of study. These colleges can supply potential applicants with the addresses of other relevant institutions. The Secretariat of the Danish Rectors' Conference can also provide the addresses of appropriate institutions.

Multi-disciplinary Universities

Københavns Universitet
(University of Copenhagen),
Nørregade 10, Postboks 2177, DK-1017 Copenhagen K
tel. +45 35 32 26 26, fax +45 35 32 26 28
www.ku.dk

Aarhus Universitet
(University of Aarhus),
Nordre Ringgade 1, DK-8000 Aarhus C,
tel. +45 89 42 11 66, fax +45 89 42 11 09,
www.aau.dk

Syddansk Universitet – Odense
(University of Southern Denmark),
Campusvej 55, DK-5230 Odense M,
tel. +45 66 15 86 00, fax +45 66 15 84 28,
www.sdu.dk

Roskilde Universitetscenter
(Roskilde University),
Postboks 260, DK-4000 Roskilde,
tel. +45 46 74 20 00, fax +45 46 74 30 00,
www.ruc.dk

Aalborg Universitet
(Aalborg University),
Postboks 159, DK-9100 Aalborg,
tel. +45 96 35 80 80, fax +45 98 15 22 01,
www.auc.dk

University Level Schools of Specialization

Danmarks Tekniske Universitet
(Technical University of Denmark),
Anker Engelundsvej 1, Bygning 101, DK-2800 Lyngby,
tel. +45 45 25 25 25, fax +45 45 88 17 99,
www.dtu.dk

Danmarks Lærerhøjskole
(Royal Danish School of Educational Studies),
Emdrupvej 101, DK-2400 Copenhagen NV,
tel. +45 39 69 66 33, fax +45 39 66 00 81,
www.dlh.dk

Den Kgl. Veterinær og Landbohøjskole
(Royal Veterinary and Agricultural University),
Bülowsvej 17, DK-1870 Frederiksberg C,
tel. +45 35 28 28 28, fax +45 35 28 20 79,
www.kvl.dk

Handelshøjskolen i København
(Copenhagen Business School),
Struenseegade 7-9, DK-2200 Copenhagen N
tel. +45 38 15 38 15, fax +45 38 15 20 15
www.cbs.dk

Handelshøjskolen i Århus
(Aarhus School of Business),
Fuglesangs Allé 4, DK-8210 Aarhus V
tel. +45 89 48 66 88, fax +45 86 15 01 88
www.hha.dk

Syddansk Universitet
Handelshøjskole Syd – Ingeniørhøjskole Syd
(Southern Denmark School of Business and Engineering;
campuses in Esbjerg, Kolding, Sønderborg, Varde and
Flensburg, Germany),
Grundtvigs Allé 150, DK-6400 Sønderborg,
tel. +45 79 32 11 11, fax +45 79 32 12 87,
www.sdu.dk

Danmarks Farmaceutiske Højskole
(Royal Danish School of Pharmacy),
Universitetsparken 2, DK-2100 Copenhagen Ø,
tel. +45 35 37 08 50, fax +45 35 37 57 44,
www.dfh.dk

Kunstakademiets Arkitektskole
(Royal Danish Academy of Fine Arts, School of Architecture),
Philip de Langes Allé 10, DK-1435 Copenhagen K,
tel. +45 32 68 60 00, fax +45 32 68 61 11
www.kulturnet.dk/homes/kaa/index-e.htm

Kunstakademiets Billedkunstskoler
(Royal Danish Academy of Fine Arts, Schools of Visual Art),
Kongens Nytorv 1, DK-1050 Copenhagen K,
tel. +45 33 74 45 00, fax +45 33 74 46 66
www.kulturnet.dk/homes/kbi

Arkitektskolen i Aarhus
(Aarhus School of Architecture),
Nørreport 20, DK-8000 Aarhus C,
tel. +45 89 36 00 00, fax +45 86 13 06 45
www.a-aarhus.dk

Det Kgl. Danske Musikkonservatorium
(Royal Danish Academy of Music),
Niels Brocks Gade 1, DK-1574 Copenhagen V,
tel. +45 33 69 22 69, fax +45 33 69 22 79
www.kulturnet.dk/homes/dkdm

Det Jyske Musikkonservatorium
(Royal Academy of Music, Aarhus),
Fuglesangs Allé 26, DK-8210 Aarhus V,
tel. +45 89 48 33 88, fax +45 89 48 33 22
www.kulturnet.dk/homes/jmk

Det Fynske Musikkonservatorium
(Carl Nielsen Academy of Music, Odense),
Islandsgade 2, DK-5000 Odense C,
tel. +45 66 11 06 63, fax +45 66 17 77 63
www.kulturnet.dk/homes/fmk

Nordjysk Musikkonservatorium
(Academy of Music, Aalborg),
Ryesgade 52, DK-9000 Aalborg,
tel. +45 98 12 77 44, fax +45 98 11 37 63
www.kulturnet.dk/homes/nmk

Vestjysk Musikkonservatorium
(Academy of Music, Esbjerg),
Islandsgade 50, DK-6700 Esbjerg,
tel. +45 75 12 61 00, fax +45 75 18 06 59
www.vmk.dk

Rytmisk Musikkonservatorium
(Rhythmic Music Conservatory),
Leo Mathisensvej, Holmen,
DK-1437 Copenhagen K,
tel. +45 32 68 67 00, fax +45 32 68 67 66
www.rmc.dk

Danmarks Journalisthøjskole
(Danish School of Journalism),
Olof Palmes Allé 11, DK-8200 Aarhus N,
tel. +45 89 44 04 40, fax +45 86 16 89 10,
www.djh.dk

Danmarks Biblioteksskole
(Royal School of Librarianship),
Birketinget 6, DK-2300 Copenhagen S,
tel. +45 31 58 60 66, fax +45 32 84 02 01,
www.db.dk

Danmarks Højskole for Legemsøvelser
(Danish State Institute of Physical Education),
Nørre Allé 51, DK-2200 Copenhagen N,
tel. +45 35 30 05 00, fax +45 35 36 24 14

Den Grafiske Højskole
(Graphic Arts Institute of Denmark),
Glentevej 67, DK-2400 Copenhagen NV,
tel. +45 38 10 11 77, fax +45 38 33 06 30,
www.dgh.dk

Danmarks Designskole
(Denmark's Design School),
Strandboulevarden 47, DK-2100 Copenhagen Ø,
tel. +45 35 27 75 00, fax +45 35 27 76 00
www.dk-designskole.dk

Den Sociale Højskole i København
(National Danish School of Social Work, Copenhagen),
Randersgade 10, DK-2100 Copenhagen Ø,
tel. +45 31 42 46 01, fax +45 31 42 07 61

Den Sociale Højskole i Århus
(National Danish School of Social Work, Aarhus),
Stenvej 4, DK-8270 Højbjerg,
tel. +45 86 27 66 22, fax +45 86 27 74 76

Den Sociale Højskole i Esbjerg
(National Danish School of Social Work, Esbjerg),
Storegade 182, DK-6705 Esbjerg Ø,
tel. +45 75 13 35 00, fax +45 75 12 09 04

Den Sociale Højskole i Odense
(National Danish School of Social Work, Odense),
Campusvej 55, DK-5230 Odense M,
tel. +45 66 15 86 00, fax +45 65 93 09 34

Colleges of Engineering

Denmark has seven colleges of engineering located in Aarhus, Copenhagen, Haslev, Herning, Horsens, Odense and Sønderborg.

The address of the college in Copenhagen is:

Københavns Teknikum
(Engineering College of Copenhagen),
Lautrupvang 15, DK-2750 Ballerup,
tel. +45 44 97 80 88, fax +45 44 97 81 72,
www.cph.ih.dk

Colleges of Education

Teacher training is offered at 18 colleges of education throughout Denmark. An example is:

Jelling Statsseminarium
(Jelling State College of Education),
Vejlevej 2, DK-7300 Jelling,
tel. +45 75 87 16 00, fax +45 75 87 12 27
www.jelllaersem.dk

Colleges of Educator Training

A total of 32 institutions train students for such occupations as preschool teachers, recreation center teachers and social educators.

One such institution is:

Viborgseminariet
(Viborg College of Educator Training),
Reberbanen 13, DK-8800 Viborg,
tel. +45 86 62 42 00, fax +45 86 61 49 09
www.viborgsem.dk

Colleges for Art, Crafts, Textile and Fashion Design

Denmark has eight of these colleges located in: Copenhagen (2), Højer, Nørre Sundby, Nykøbing Falster, Odense, Kerteminde and Skals.

One example is:

Hellerup Håndarbejdsseminarium
(Hellerup College for Art, Crafts, Textile and Fashion Design),
Frederikkevej 810, DK-2900 Hellerup,
tel. +45 39 61 93 93, fax +45 39 61 97 97

Health Education Institutions

Nursing (22 schools)

Hovedstadens Sygehusfællesskab, Sygeplejerskeuddannelsen,
Tuborgvej 235, DK-2400 Copenhagen NV,
tel. +45 35 31 36 93, fax +45 35 31 24 67

Medical Laboratory Technicians (2 schools)

Hospitalslaborantskolen i Århus
(School for Medical Laboratory Technicians in Aarhus),
Studsgade 29, DK-8000 Aarhus C,
tel. +45 86 12 63 66, fax +45 86 12 62 08

Midwifery

(2 departments: Copenhagen and Aalborg)

Danmarks Jordemoderskole
(Danish Midwifery School – Copenhagen Department),
Rigshospitalet, afsnit 7211,
Tagensvej 18, DK-2200 Copenhagen N,
tel. +45 35 45 72 16, fax +45 35 36 18 10

Occupational Therapists (6 schools)

Ergoterapeutskolen i Århus
(School of Occupational Therapy in Aarhus),
Skejbyvej 15, DK-8240 Risskov,
tel. +45 86 21 16 11, fax +45 86 21 29 12

Physiotherapists (8 schools)

Fysioterapeutskolen i Århus
(School of Physiotherapy in Aarhus),
Skejbyvej 15, DK-8240 Risskov,
tel. +45 86 21 14 55, fax +45 86 21 29 12

Summer courses

Det Danske Kulturinstitut
(Danish Cultural Institute),
Kultorvet 2, DK-1175 Copenhagen K,
tel. +45 33 13 54 48, fax +45 33 15 10 91

Den Internationale Højskole
(International People's College),
Montebello Allé, DK-3000 Helsingør,
tel. +45 49 21 33 61, fax +45 49 21 21 28

Handelshøjskolen (Copenhagen Business School)
International Graduate Summer University Program
International Office
Dalgas Have 15, DK-2000 Frederiksberg
tel. +45 38 15 30 06, fax +45 38 15 38 25
www.cbs.dk/adm/dik/summer

International Exchange Programs

All Danish institutions of higher education are involved in international programs. A large number of student exchanges are arranged under bilateral agreements between a Danish institution and a foreign partner university.

For more information contact:

Rektorkollegiets Sekretariat
(Secretariat of the Danish Rectors' Conference),
H C Andersens Boulevard 45, DK-1553 Copenhagen V,
tel. +45 33 92 54 06, fax +45 33 92 50 75
www.rks.dk

The Secretariat is responsible for administration in Denmark of the European Union programs for higher education (Socrates/Erasmus, Leonardo da Vinci (in co-operation with ACIU), Tempus, and the NARIC center on academic recognition) and the cultural agreement programs.

ICU – Informationscenter for Udveksling
(Information Centre for Exchange),
Vandkunsten 3, DK-1467 Copenhagen K,
tel. +45 33 14 20 60, fax +45 33 14 36 40

The Center is Denmark's agency for the following European Union programs: Socrates/Comenius, Socrates/Chapter III, CEDEFOP, Youth for Europe and Action for Voluntary Service as well as for the Ministry of Education's Visitors' Service.

Other relevant addresses

Udenrigsministeriet
(Ministry of Foreign Affairs),
Asiatisk Plads 2, DK-1448 Copenhagen K,
tel. +45 33 92 00 00, fax +45 31 54 05 33
www.um.dk

Undervisningsministeriet,
(Ministry of Education),
Frederiksholms Kanal 26, DK-1220 Copenhagen K,
tel. +45 33 92 50 00, fax +45 33 92 55 67,
www.uvm.dk/eng

Undervisningsministeriet, Universitetsafdelingen,
(Ministry of Education, Department of Higher Education),
H C Andersens Boulevard 40,
DK-1553 Copenhagen V,
tel. +45 33 92 53 00, fax +45 33 92 53 25
www.uvm.dk/eng.htm

Kulturministeriet (Ministry of Cultural Affairs),
Nybrogade 2, DK-1203 Copenhagen K,
tel. +45 33 92 33 70, fax +45 33 91 33 88

Forskerakademiet (Danish Research Academy),
Observatorievejen 3, DK-8000 Aarhus C,
tel. +45 86 14 48 99, fax +45 86 14 48 71,
www.danphd.dk

Denmark's International Study Program (DiS),
Vestergade 7, DK-1456 Copenhagen K,
tel. +45 33 11 01 44, fax +45 33 93 26 24,
www.disp.dk

DanmarkAmerika Fondet/Fulbright Kommissionen
(DenmarkAmerica Foundation/Fulbright Commission),
Fiolstræde 24, 3. sal, DK-1171 Copenhagen K,
tel. +45 33 12 82 23, fax +45 33 32 53 23

Udlændingestyrelsen (Danish Immigration Service),
Ryesgade 53, DK-2100 Copenhagen Ø,
tel. +45 35 36 66 00, fax +45 35 36 50 29
www.udlst.dk

Appendix 4: Accommodations

Student Housing

The educational institutions have practically no residential facilities of their own, and both Danish and non-Danish students normally have to make their own arrangements. Nevertheless, some of the major cities have student dormitories and other housing facilities coordinated regionally by:

Centralindstillingsudvalget,
H C Andersens Boulevard 13, DK-1553 Copenhagen V,
tel. +45 33 11 64 44, fax +45 33 11 17 27

Roskilde regionale indstillingsudvalg,
Parkvej 5, DK-4000 Roskilde,
tel. +45 42 36 22 02

RIUFyn, Hinderupgård,
Niels Bohrs Allé 21, DK-5230 Odense M,
tel. +45 66 13 40 08, fax +45 65 90 61 77

Indstillingsudvalget for Aalborg Kollegier (IFAK),
Nyhavnsgade 15, Postboks 1713, DK-9000 Aalborg,
tel. +45 98 13 44 30, fax + 45 99 31 27 99

Kollegiekontoret i Århus (AMBA),
Vesterport 1, st., DK-8000 Aarhus C,
tel. +45 86 13 21 66, fax +45 86 13 21 80

Faculty Housing

Most universities and colleges have guest apartments that visiting professors and researcher can rent for short term stays in Denmark. These apartments are often situated close to the institution and maintained well. Contact your host for more information regarding the availability of housing.

Below are a couple of addresses of relocation services in Denmark.

Copenhagen Relocations
Halls Allé 13, DK-1802 Frederiksberg C
Tel. +45 33 79 72 19

Home from Home Relocation Services
Strandvejen 203, DK-2900 Hellerup
tel. +45 70 22 40 00, fax +45 70 22 60 00
e-mail: info@hfh-relocations.dk
hyperlink http://www.hfh-relocations.dk

Appendix 5: Glossary

amt — county
børnehave — pre-school
børnehaveklasse — kindergarten
candidatus — master's level degree
dagpleje — in-home daycare
dankort — Danish debit card
Folkeregisteret — Civil Registrar's Office
Folketinget — the Parliament
fredagsbar — Friday's bar
fritidshjem — after school recreation center
fritidsklub — after-school clubs
gymnasium — upper secondary school /high school
hygge — warmth, comfort, coziness
Internordisk flyttebevis — Inter-Nordic Certificate of Change of Address
Janteloven — The Law of Jante
julefrokost — Christmas lunch
kollegium — residence hall / dormitory
kommune — municipality
krone — crown (Danish monetary unit)
legestue — child/parent activity center
mf (midt for) — in the middle (in an address)
møntkort — cash card
natmad — midnight snack
pasningsordning — child care arrangement
rugbrød — rye bread
skål — cheers

smørrebrød	open-faced sandwiches
snaps	Danish aquavit (liquor)
st (stuen)	ground floor
statsministeren	Prime Minister
student	upper secondary school graduate
studentereksamen	upper secondary school exit exams
sygesikringsbevis	national health insurance card
søskenderabat	sibling rebate
tak for mad	thank you for the meal
th (til højre)	to the right (in an address)
told og skatteregioner	regional tax zones
tv (til venstre)	to the left (in an address)
vuggestue	daycare center
øl	beer
øre	coin worth 1/100 of a *krone*

References

Dahlgaard, G. (Ed.). (1996). *Short cuts: Do's and don'ts in Copenhagen – a guide*. Copenhagen: Ungdomsinformationen København.

Den Store Danske Encyklopædi, volume 4. (1996). Copenhagen: Danmarks Nationalleksikon A/S.

Kjersgaard, E. (1982). Kjersgaards Danmarkshistorie 1, 2, 3. Copenhagen: Forlaget Komma A/S.

MacHaffie, I. S. & Nielsen, M. A. (1976). *Of Danish Ways*. Minneapolis. MN: Dillon Press.

Scocozza, B. & Jensen. (1994). *Danmarkshistoriens: Hvem Hvad og Hvornår*. Copenhagen: Politikens Forlag A/S.

Secretariat of the Danish Rectors' Conference, (1997). *Internationalisation of higher education in Denmark: A debate outline*. Copenhagen: Author.

Secretariat of the Danish Rectors' Conference. (1994). *Higher education in Denmark: A guide for foreign students and institutions of higher education*. Copenhagen: Author.

Thomas, F. R. (Ed.). (1990). *Americans in Denmark: Comparisons of the two cultures by writers, artists, and teachers*. Southern Illinois University Press.

Oxford Research. (1998). *The Expat-Study '98*. Copenhagen: Author.

Ministry of Economics. (1994). *Kvinder i økonomien. (Women in the economy)*. Copenhagen: Author.